CATHOLIC UNIVERSITY OF AMERICA
STUDIES IN CANON LAW
No. 46

—

CONDEMNED SOCIETIES

A DISSERTATION

SUBMITTED TO THE FACULTY OF CANON LAW OF THE
CATHOLIC UNIVERSITY OF AMERICA IN PARTIAL
FULFILMENT OF THE REQUIREMENTS FOR THE
DEGREE OF DOCTOR IN CANON LAW

BY

JOSEPH A. M. QUIGLEY, A.B., J.C.L.

Priest of the Archdiocese of Philadelphia

CATHOLIC UNIVERSITY OF AMERICA
WASHINGTON, D. C.
1927

Nihil Obstat

Washingtonii, die 7 Maii, 1927

✝ Thomas J. Shahan, S.T.D., J.U.L.

Episcopus Germanicopolis

Censor Deputatus

Imprimatur

Philadelphiae, die 7 Maii, 1927

✝ D. Card. Dougherty

Archiepiscopus Philadelphiensis

FOREWORD

THE question of condemned societies has been thrusting itself upon us for many years, and is daily increasing in importance. Of one condemned society alone, the aggregate membership throughout the world is rated at four and one half millions, two-thirds of whom are in the United States.

Everywhere we turn the strength and influence of condemned societies is evident: we rub elbows constantly with their members. Moreover, priests in the fulfillment of their sacred ministry are continually meeting canonical problems relative to the members of condemned societies. So far as can be ascertained, there has never been written, as yet, at least in English, a canonical monograph on this interesting, but perplexing subject.

It has, therefore, been the aim of the writer of this treatise to collect into one volume the Canon Law on condemned societies. He has attempted to answer, dispassionately and fairly, the many difficulties that may present themselves, not only to the priest on the mission, but also to the canonist in the diocesan chancery.

The writer takes this opportunity of expressing his deep gratitude to the Faculty of Canon Law at the Catholic University for the timely interest and unfailing kindness shown him in the preparation of this work.

3

TABLE OF CONTENTS

CHAPTER I

DEFINITION AND DIVISION OF CONDEMNED SOCIETIES

A CONDEMNED society is one in which the Church forbids her subjects to take membership, or which she declares illicit. This interpretation in the extra-judicial sense of the term " damnare " is justified by the use of the word in the official documents of the Holy See, as shall be seen below. Hence what some writers would call a merely prohibited society is in reality a condemned society. To prohibit membership in a society, or to declare that society unlawful, is to condemn it, whether or not a sanction is added to the prohibition.

The Church condemns in general all societies that pursue an evil end, or make use of evil means to attain an end, no matter how good in itself, or that are likely to prove a source of perversion, moral or doctrinal, to the faithful.[1]

Condemned societies, for practical purposes, may be divided according to their nature, the manner of their condemnation, and the sanction attached to their condemnation. According to their nature, they are Anti-Social, Secret, Bible, Cremation and Theosophical Societies. According to the manner of their condemnation, they are societies condemned *nominatim*, or by name, and societies condemned implicitly. According to the sanction attached to their condemnation, they are societies condemned under censure, and societies condemned without censure, but *sub gravi*.

Anti-Social Societies are those that conspire, or plot, against either the Church, or State, or both. They are

---

[1] Genicot-Salsmans, *Inst. Theo. Mor.*, II, p. 291, No. 359, bis.

7

"adversus societatem ecclesiasticam, vel civilem": hence their name "Anti-Social".

Secret societies are organizations, the members of which are bound to secrecy concerning their constitutions, purposes, means, degree work, and the like. In the past a secret society was understood to be one whose existence was known, but whose members, their number, and their places of meeting were unknown.[2]

Now, however, a secret society is one that completely conceals from the uninitiated its rules, usages, passwords, symbols, ritual and regalia. An oath of inviolate secrecy is usually demanded, and, sometimes, even of blind obedience to unknown leaders.[3]

Although it is not the practice of writers to distinguish between Secret Societies and Anti-Social Societies that are secret, calling them all Secret Societies, still in the pages that follow this distinction will be strictly adhered to, for the sake of clearness, not to mention correctness. Könings well remarks: "patet damnatas societates 'improprie' tantum dici posse 'occultas' seu 'secretas'".[4]

Bible Societies are associations founded for the purpose of translating the Sacred Scriptures, publishing them "without note or comment,"[5] rejecting usually the Deutero-Canonical Books as apocryphal, and distributing the Bibles at cost, less than cost, or gratis. Their operations are carried on all over the world by means of colportage, and their agents are known as colporteurs, or, less elegantly, Bible-hawkers. They are naturally a Protestant effort, the outcome of the

[2] Rosen, *The Catholic Church and Secret Societies*, p. 11.

[3] Raich, "Freimaurerei" *Kirchenlexikon*, V, p. 519.

[4] *Theo. Mor.*, II, p. 346, No. 1721.

[5] Cf. Constitution of the American Bible Society, contained in Dwight. *The Centential History of the Amercian Bible Society*, I, p. 25.

Protestant doctrine of private judgment, and the rejection of Tradition.

Cremation Societies are associations whose purpose is the furtherance of the practice of cremation. These societies pursue their end in many ways. They broadcast information concerning cremation, and its supposed advantages over inhumation. They carry on a kind of insurance, by which, for a small sum payable annually, cremation is secured after death. They erect and maintain costly crematories, and their members, naturally, pledge themselves to have their bodies turned over after death for cremation.

Theosophical Societies are both religious sects and secret societies. Their purpose, according to Mrs. Annie Besant, is to " form a nucleus of the Universal Brotherhood of Humanity without distinction of race, creed, sex, caste, or color : to encourage the study of comparative religion, philosophy and science : to investigate unexplained laws of nature, and the powers latent in man ".[6] The magic, the occult, the uncanny, and the marvelous, in any and every form, are included in the last clause of Mrs. Besant's definition.[7] There is an esoteric section to which only members of a year's standing are admitted, and which is admittedly a secret society.[8] As religious sects, Theosophical Societies will be of no interest here, but only in their character of secret societies.[9]

Societies condemned *nominatim,* or nominally, are those explicitly condemned by name : societies condemned implicitly

[6] Besant, Mrs. Annie, " Theosophy ", Hasting's *Encyclopedia of Religion and Ethics,* XII, p. 303.

[7] Driscoll, " Theosophy ", *Cath. Ency.,* XIV, p. 627.

[8] Preuss, *Dict. of Secret and Other Societies,* p. 456. This is an opportune work, and fills a long-felt need.

[9] Cf. Cerato, *Censurae Vigentes,* p. 109, No. 2 : Cipollini, *De Censuris Latae Sententiae,* p. 134.

are those comprehended in the general condemnation of condemned societies, those societies that have in them the notes set apart by law as numbering a society among condemned societies.

Societies condemned under censure are those which it is forbidden to join under pain of excommunication. " Nomen dantes ... contrahunt ipso facto excommunicationem ".[10]

Societies condemned without censure, but *sub gravi,* are those which the Church has declared unlawful, and, consequently, has prohibited her children to join under pain of mortal sin.[11]

[10] Canon 2335.

[11] Cf. S. C. S. Off., 10 Maii, 1884, *C. I. C. Fontes,* IV, p. 428, No. 1100.

CHAPTER II

THE CONDEMNATION OF CONDEMNED SOCIETIES

ARTICLE I.   THE CONDEMNATION OF ANTI-SOCIAL SOCIETIES

ANTI-SOCIAL societies are found for the first time in the consolidation of four guilds, or lodges of stone-masons into the first Lodge of Free and Accepted Masons, an event that took place in London as late as June 24, 1717.   This society, or, rather, this system of international brotherhoods, as it has now become, the result of that first meeting in an obscure London tavern, is the classical example of this species of condemned societies.   The history of its condemnation, together with that of the Carbonari, and Fenians, the other two nominally condemned anti-social societies, is identified with the subject of this first article.

The Freemasons spread rapidly over Europe, and crossed the seas to the colonies of America, and even to far Hindustan, in little more than a score of years after the inception of their fraternity.[1]   The true nature of the organization at once declared itself.   But it seems rather strange that the craft, in the beginning, should have been protected by a Catholic Power, when Protestant governments were condemning it.   Francis I of Austria[2] was its patron and protector, while Holland, Sweden, Hamburg and Geneva were taking action against it.[3]

[1] Cooper, Reprint from *Amer. Eccl. Review*, " Freemasonry's Two Hundredth Birthday ", June, 1917, p. 591.

[2] Gruber, " Masonry ", *Cath. Ency.*, IX, p. 786.

[3] Gautherot, " Franc-Maçonnerie ", *Dict. Apol. de la Foi Cath.*, VII, col. 127.

It was not till the year 1738 that the Holy See saw fit to condemn Freemasonry.[4]   The Holy See was not ignorant of the existence of the craft, of its character and malice, and of the danger both to the good of souls and the state lurking in it.   But just as in the century following many years elapsed from the time Bishop Kenrick first asked the Propaganda about the Odd Fellows to their nominal condemnation by the Holy Office, so the reigning Pontiff, Clement XII, weighing well the facts of the case, gave his sentence only after mature deliberation.   He was moved thereto, not by impulse, but by reason.   And even when the condemnation was finally pronounced, there were not a few thoughtless Catholics who were surprised at the Pontiff's attitude.   They did not know, as he did, the religious indifference and the disrespect for authority and truth the sect insinuated, not only into the hearts and minds of its sectaries, but also of all those with whom it came in contact.   What was behind their " secret work ", the malice and iniquity of their oath of inviolate secrecy and of blind obedience, were patent, not so much to the simple-minded, as to those who were able to judge the society along Christian, social and political standards.[5]

To exterminate this " scourge of God ", Clement XII condemned Freemasonry in his constitution "In Eminenti ", April 28, 1738.[6]   He imposed " excommunicationem latae sententiae uni Romano Pontifici reservatam . . . tum in nomen dantes Sectis Masonicis, tum in eos qui eiusmodi sectis consilium, auxilium, favorem quomodolibet praestarent ".[7] And he ordered and empowered all Ordinaries, Major Pre-

---

[4] Constitution "In Eminenti", of Clement XII, 28 June, 1738, *C. I. C. Fontes*, I, p. 656, No. 299.

[5] Cf. Leech, *Comparative Study of the Const. Apos. Sed. and C. I. C.*, p. 58: Gruber, "Masonry", *Cath. Ency.*, IX, p. 786.

[6] *C. I. C. Fontes*, I, p. 656, No. 299.

[7] Pennacchi, *Commentaria in Const. Apos. Sedis*, I, p. 598.

lates and Deputy Inquisitors " contra haereticam pravitatem "
to summon, try and punish the Masons as those gravely suspected of heresy, and, if need be, to call in the civil authorities
to carry out his commands.

Although this solemn anathema against the Masons was
never revoked,[8] there were some persons who declared after
Clement's death, and the accession of Cardinal Lambertini
as Benedict XIV, that the condemnation and censure contained in " In Eminenti " was no longer in force because the
new Pontiff had never renewed, or confirmed it.[9]

Benedict XIV himself later declared that even if he had
never in so many words condemned and censured the Freemasons, he had, nevertheless, at least negatively given assent
and confirmation to the constitution of his predecessor. He
further declared that a constitution passed by one Pope did
not need the confirmation of his successor to be binding in
law.[10] He accordingly promulgated the constitution " Providas ", which " reproduit cette (constitution) de Clement
XII, et condamne à nouveau le naturalisme, le caractère
secret, le serment et les tendances révolutionnaires de la
secte ".[11] The Pope gave as the reasons of the condemnation of the Masons what Clement XII had hinted at, religious
indifference, absolute secrecy, the oath of secrecy, and disrespect for civil and ecclesiastical authority, and he added
two reasons of his own, the fact that so many civil governments had already condemned the craft, and that the joining
of it was considered by men of prudence and merit an act of
depravity and perversion.

[8] Darras, *General History of the Cath. Church*, IV, p. 471.

[9] Parsons, *Studies in Church History*, IV, p. 411.

[10] Constitution " Providas " May 18, 412, paragraphs 3-5, *C. I. C.
Fontes*, II, p. 316, No. 412.

[11] Gautherot, " Franc-Maçonnerie ", *Dict. Apol. de la Foi Cath.*, VII,
col. 127, *C. I. C. Fontes*, II, p. 315, No. 412.

It will be noted that Pope Benedict added nothing to the existing legislation; he confirmed what Clement had already ordained, which, as Pennacchi puts it, " Praeclarissimis sententiis illustraverit ".[12]

From 1751 to 1821 there were no further Papal pronouncements against anti-social societies, though Pius VI in his encyclical " Inscrutabile", published December 25, 1775,[13] had fulminated against the philosophy and the revolutionary teachings of Freemasonry, without, however, nominally mentioning the sect.[14]

In the last quarter of the eighteenth century there arose in Italy a society that was soon to spread far and wide in that land, cross the Alps into France, and then cross the Pyrenees into Spain. It was called the Carbonari, or Charcoal-Burners. Initiation into the sect was accomplished by an unspeakable mockery of the Sacred Passion of Our Lord, the sectaries bound themselves by a terrible oath to the strictest silence and secrecy, and in it pledged themselves as ready to accept the direst punishments for its violation. Their openly admitted purpose was to bring about either a constitutional monarchy, or a republic, and their means proved to be assassination and armed rebellion.[15] In their sedition, they pushed their way into the States of the Church, and attempted to overthrow the temporal dominion of the Papacy: " atque Sedem hanc Apostolicam evertant, in quam, quoniam in ea Apostolica Cathedra semper viguit principatus, singulari quodam odio afficiuntur, ut pestifera quaeque ac perniciosa moliuntur ".[16]

[12] *Com. in Const. Apos. Sed.,* I, p. 602.

[13] *C. I. C. Fontes,* II, p. 649, No. 470.

[14] Gautherot, " Franc-Maçonnerie ", *Dict. Apol. de la Foi Cath.,* VII, col. 127.

[15] Kirsch, " Carbonari ", *Cath. Ency.,* III, p. 330.

[16] Const. " Ecclesiam ", Pius VII, September 13, 1821, *C. I. C. Fontes,* II, p. 723, No. 479.

On morality they taught that it was permitted to do away with those who had violated the oath of secrecy, and to assassinate kings and other rulers, whom they indiscriminately termed tyrants, although the sect claimed it practised both charity and virtue.

Pius VII, that long-suffering and much persecuted Pontiff, could not observe further silence; he was forced to raise his voice against the Carbonari and their outrages. He, therefore, in a constitution, "Ecclesiam", given September 15, 1821, condemned the Carbonari forever and all their "vendette". He repeated the constitution "In Eminenti" and "Providas", applying them to this sect, "ut nihil de eiusmodi Pontificia sanctione praemittere pariter putemus." [17] He commanded that no one, no matter what his rank, dignity, or preëminence, join, favor, or aid the Carbonari, under any pretext, under pain of excommunication reserved to the Apostolic See. He introduced the obligation binding all the faithful of denouncing to the proper authorities, under pain of the same censure, all known to have joined, or favored the sect, and he condemned all their books and writings, printed and in manuscript, and prohibited the faithful "sub eadem poena maioris excommunicationis eodem modo reservatae" to read or retain these writings in their possession, commanding that they be delivered to the Ordinaries, or to clerics delegated for the purpose.[18]

By no means were the anti-social sectaries daunted by the foregoing condemnations of the Roman Pontiffs. Their arrogance increased day by day, due to the multiplication of new societies. The Church was everywhere the prey of the bitterest calamities. Her dogmas and precepts were assailed; her dignity belittled; the peace and tranquility that were hers

---

[17] Pennacchi, *Com. in Const. Apos. Sed.*, I, p. 606.

[18] *C. I. C. Fontes*, II, p. 721, No. 479.

by divine right were destroyed. The anti-social societies were the cause of all this and much more. They spurned authority, blasphemed majesty, taught there was no God, denied the immortality of the soul, made a scandal of Christ and a folly. These accusations were not rashly made. The constitutions, statutes, rituals, and other literature of the sects manifested that they professed all that was laid at their doors, " quae ad legitimos principatus labefactandos et Ecclesiam funditus delendam spectant ".[19]

Shortly after his election, Leo XII turned his attention to the anti-social societies, and attempted to find their number, status, and influence. He felt it his duty to condemn again these societies, and to condemn them in such a way that it would be impossible to claim exemption from the condemnation. He therefore issued the constitution " Quo Graviora ", March 13, 1825, in which he inserted and expressly confirmed the three previous constitutions.[20]

The Pontiff perpetually condemned all societies, then existing, or which ever might exist, and which would set themselves against the Church, or State, and he forbade under censure any one to join, propagate, favor, aid, or counsel them; he extended the obligation of denouncing under censure the members and *fautores* of the Carbonari to that of denouncing, also under censure, the members and favorers of all anti-social societies. Condemning the secret societies springing up at the universities,[21] he pointed out the iniquity of the oath taken in such societies, and asked the civil rulers to punish the anti-social conspirators who were no less the

[19] Cf. Leo XII, const. " Quo Graviora ", paragraphs 10-13, March 13, 1825, *C. I. C. Fontes,* II, p. 733, No. 481. Cf. Also: Pike, *Morals and Dogma,* etc., p. 50, 69, 70, 74, 149, 164, 823-824.

[20] Gautherot, " Franc-Maçonnerie ", *Dict. Apol. de la Foi Cath.,* VII, col. 127, gives the year as 1826.

[21] Cf. Fanning, " Secret Societies ", *Cath. Ency.,* XIV, p. 74.

enemies of the state than they were of the Church, and he exhorted the faithful to shun these societies entirely.[22]

Finally the Pope relaxed for a year the reservation of the censure, and the obligation of denunciation, and allowed any confessor, even those in Rome, to absolve the anti-social sectaries, and their abbettors.[23]

Pius VIII succeeded Leo XII, but reigned for only a year and six months; he found time, however, in his short reign to confirm the condemnation of the Masons and like societies in the encyclical " Traditi ", May 21, 1829.[24]   Just as Leo XII had condemned the secret societies at the universities, so did Pius VIII condemn those at the colleges and academies. He exhorted the Bishops to do all in their power to drive these societies out of their dioceses, and he begged them to strive with all the authority and grace they could muster that none but men of virtue and learning be entrusted with the education of youth.

Gregory XVI addressed an encyclical to all Bishops of the Catholic world, " Mirari Vos ", of August 15, 1832.[25] In it he " revient à son tour sur ce sujet, compare les sociétés secrètes à ' un cloaque ' dans lequel ' sont entassées et amalgamées les souillures de tout ce qu'il y a eu de sacrilège, d'infame, de blasphématoire, dans les hérésies et les sectes les plus scélérates ' ".[26]

It is usually the case that a certain bull of Pope Gregory's

[22] Gautherot, " Franc-Maçonnerie ", *Dict. Apol. de la Foi Cath.*, VII, col. 127.

[23] Alzog says that the constitution " Quo Graviora " was perhaps less opportune than " Ubi Primum " which condemned Bible Societies. Cf. *Universal History of the Cath. Church*, IV, p. 62, note 2, for controversy.

[24] *Bullarii Romani Continuatio*, XIV, p. 23.

[25] *C. I. C. Fontes*, II, p. 744, No. 485.

[26] Gautherot, " Franc-Maçonnerie ", *Dict. Apol. de la Foi Cath.*, VII, col. 127.

termed " Inter ", is cited as against Freemasonry and anti-social socieites.[27]   This Pontiff wrote two encyclicals beginning "Inter".   One of them, "Inter Gravissimas", treated of certain questions relative to the Armenian Uniates;[28] the other, " Inter Praecipuas ", condemned Bible Societies and the Christian Alliance.[29]   More probably it is this latter to which reference is made.   However, this quotation seems to be rather inaccurate.

Pius IX inaugurated his long strife against anti-social societies by the encyclical " Qui Pluribus ", of November 9, 1846, in which he confirmed their condemnation.[30] He again condemned them in an allocution, " Quibus Quantisque ", terming them " abominabiles perditionis sectas, non solum animarum saluti, verum etiam civilis societatis bono ac tranquilitati vel maxime infestas ".[31]   Anti-social societies were also mentioned as the principles among the " impium incredulorum genus, qui omnem si fieri posset exterminatum vellent religionis cultum " in another allocution, " Singulari Quidem ", delivered December 9, 1854.[32]   In still another allocution, " Maxima Quidem ", the Pontiff again referred to the persecution of the Church, the denial of Catholic truth, and the blasphemies against God and His Church, of which the anti-social sects were guilty,[33] and in a brief addressed to Msgr. Darby, Archbishop of Paris, and a victim of the Commune, he declared:—

Ces sectes coalissés forment la synagogue de Satan. . . .

[27] Cf. Pennacchi, *Com. in Const. Apos. Sed.*, I, p. 613: Leech, *Comparative Study of Const. Apos. Sed.*, and *C. I. C.* p. 58.

[28] February 23, 1832, *C. I. C. Fontes*, II, p. 736, No. 483.

[29] May 5, 1844, C. I. C. Fontes, II, p. 797, No. 502.

[30] *C. I. C. Fontes*, II, p. 807, No. 504.

[31] April 20, 1849, *C. I. C. Fontes*, 823, No. 507.

[32] *C. I. C. Fontes*, II, p. 891, No. 518.

[33] June 9, 1862, *C. I. C. Fontes*, II, p. 962, No. 534.

Elles ont enfin ce à quoi elles aspirent, constate la dernière encyclique. . . . En possession de la force et de l'autorité, elles tournent audacieusement leurs efforts à reduire l'Eglise de Dieu à la plus dure servitude. Elles voudraient, si c'etait possible, la faire disparaitre de l'univers.[34]

About this time some Liberalists were teaching that the laws of the Church did not oblige in conscience unless promulgated by the civil government, and, therefore, the condemnation of the Freemasons, and the censure under which they labored, had no force where the civil authorities tolerated the lodges. Pius IX accordingly condemned this opinion in his encyclical " Quanta Cura ", December 8, 1864.[35]

On September 25, 1865, Pope Pius IX again condemned the Masons, Carbonari and kindred sects in his allocution " Multiplices Inter ", and he again reproved the opinion that the Apostolic Constitutions condemning these societies have no force in countries where these fraternities were tolerated by the civil government.[36]

In the course of time much confusion had arisen concerning censures in general, and particularly, concerning censures " latae sententiae ". Some of the censures decreed in the past had lost their usefulness, and many doubts presented themselves to the faithful and their pastors concerning them. To meet these difficulties, Pius IX, October 12, 1869, promulgated the constitution " Apostolicae Sedis Moderationi ", which was to fix *taxative* all censures *latae sententiae*, to be thereafter binding, abolishing all constituted prior to that time and not contained in the constitution. Among the simply reserved to the Holy See we find the following :—

---

[34] October 26, 1865, Gautherot, "Franc-Maçonnerie", *Dict. Apol. de la Foi Cath.*, VII, col. 127.

[35] *C. I. C. Fontes*, II, p. 993, No. 542.

[36] *C. I. C. Fontes*, II, p. 1009, No. 554.

Nomen dantes sectae Massonicae aut Carbonariae, aut aliis eiusdem generis sectis, quae contra Ecclesiam vel legitimas potestates seu palam se clandestine machinantur, nec non iisdem sectis favorem qualemcunque praestantes; earumve occultos coriphaeos ac duces non denunciantes, donec non denunciaverint.[37]

Hence all those who joined the Masons, or the Carbonari, or other sects of the same kind, were still excommunicated *ipso facto,* as were the *fautores* of these sects. The obligation of denunciation was restricted to that of denouncing the occult leaders of the societies, and the reservation of the censure for not denouncing bound only *donec non denunciaverint.*[38] Pennacchi thinks, and so do many others who followed him, that *eiusdem genus* means Masonic in rite, secrecy, form, procedure, and the like;[39] but Lega rightly says, as shall be seen below, that the *genus* of societies condemned and censured by this number of "Apostolicae Sedis", or, rather, societies *eiusdem generis,* will be discerned "ex fine, seu ex proposito machinandi contra Ecclesiam aut legitimam potestatem, nempe civilem politicam ".[40]

The feasibility of this obligation of denouncing the occult leaders under pain of *ipso facto* excommunication was demonstrated by the Holy Office to the Vicar Apostolic of Mysore in India. The prelate had hinted that there was no good to be obtained from this obligation, " quod nomina praesedentium et membra cuiusque, ' logiae ' publice typis dantur ". The Sacred Congregation answered February, 1, 1871, that even though these names might be made public,

---

[37] *C. I. C. Fontes,* III, p. 27, No. 552.

[38] Pennacchi, *Com. in Const. Apos. Sed.,* I, p. 615.

[39] Pennacchi, *Com. in Const. Apos. Sed.,* I, 618.

[40] Lega, *Praelectiones in Text. Iur. Can.,* IV, p. 68.

nevertheless " quis sane dicere aut nosse valeat, utrum qui in publicis ephemeridis appareant, specie tantum ac nomine tenus coriphaei ac duces sint, vere autem machinationum artifices directoresque diletescant ".[41]

In the encyclical " Etsi Multa " Pius IX made his last stand against the Freemasons and similar condemned societies. He deplored the secret warfare they were carrying on against the Church, and he exhorted the Bishops to guard their flocks against the ravages of these sects, and to try to convert those who had been led away by them. The Bishops were also to disillusion all who pleaded the social and convivial benefits as their excuse for joining. And the Pope found it necessary to declare again expressly that not only were the Masons in Europe affected by the Pontifical condemnation and censure of the sect, but also those in America, " aliisque totius orbis plagis ".[42]

Pope Leo XIII wrote five encyclicals against the Masons; they are " Etsi Nos ", of February 15, 1882,[43] " Humanum Genus ", of April 20, 1882,[44] " Dall 'Alto ",[45] of October 15, 1890, " Praeclara ", of June 20, 1894,[46] and " Annum Ingressi ".[47] These encyclicals for the most part take up the different doctrines and tenets as well as the movements and tendencies of the anti-social societies, and in particular of the

[41] *C. I. C. Fontes,* IV, p. 319, No. 1014.

[42] November 21, 1873, *C. I. C. Fontes,* III, p. 77, No. 566. "Exponite eis saepe et altius animis defigite, Pontificias de re Constitutiones et docete non unos ab illis percelli masonicos coetus in Europa constitutos, sed omnes quotquot in America, aliisque totius orbis plagis habentur."

[43] *C. I. C. Fontes,* III, p. 186, No. 583.

[44] *C. I. C. Fontes,* III, p. 221, No. 591; cf. *Great Encyclicals of Leo, XIII,* p. 83.

[45] *C. I. C. Fontes,* III, p. 344, No. 609.

[46] *C. I. C. Fontes,* III, p. 441, No. 625.

[47] March 19, 1902. *Acta Sanctae Sedis,* XXXIV, p. 513; given in Italian.

Freemasons, pointing out their malice, exhorting the faithful to avoid them, and suggesting, as in the case of " Humanum Genus ", a remedy. There is, however, little of canonical interest, other than that by them the condemnation of these societies was, at least, implicitly renewed.

The new Code of Canon Law carries these condemnations of anti-social societies in Canons 684, 2335, and 2336, which canons will be seen below in their proper place.

The Fenians

Among the many patriotic associations that sprung up in Ireland in the early part of last century, there is one that is of considerable interest as the example of an anti-social society condemned, not by Pontifical decree, but by a decision of the Holy Office, namely the Irish-American association known as the Fenian Brotherhood.

The Fenians were founded in the United States, in the city of New York, and despite the claims of many Fenians the brotherhood was a secret organization,[48] at least in Ireland, and also anti-social in character. The organization, as was admitted in a convention held in Chicago, November, 1863, had as its object the separation of Ireland and Canada from England, and both countries were to set up as independent republics.[49] The Fenians, although not intent on the overthrow of the Church, by their very constitution opposed and conspired against the British Government. They did not consider the British rule as a *potestas legitima,* and hence claimed that they were not embraced by the general condemnation of anti-social societies and the censure under which they were condemned.

---

[48] Savage, *Fenian Heroes and Martyrs,* p. 58; O'Leary, *Recollections of Fenians and Fenianism,* I, pp. 120-121; Pollard, *The Secret Societies of Ireland,* p. 58.

[49] Pollard, *The Secret Societies of Ireland,* p. 58.

The Irish Hierarchy arose against the movement of the Brotherhood, and in 1861 no Fenian could receive absolution, unless he quit the society.[50]

Now the matter was brought to the attention of the Holy Office, and accordingly that Congregation decided that its decree of August 5, 1846 applied to the Fenians and the Society of St. Patrick.[51]

This decree of August 5, 1846, was in answer to a question proposed by certain Bishops of North America, " quaenam sint societates damnatae in pontificiis constitutionibus ". As will be seen later, the response did not answer the question. It did however emphasize the fact that for a society to be condemned under censure, conspiracy against either Church or state was sufficient, and that conspiracy against both was not required. In other words, that the " vel " or the phrase " adversus Ecclesiam vel gubernium " was disjunctive.[52]

When, therefore, the Holy Office replied, July 5, 1865, that this decree was against the Fenians, the conclusion was that although the Fenians might not be conspiring against the Church, since they were conspiring against the British Government of Ireland, and Canada, they were condemned and subject to the censure.

Moreover, less than a fortnight later, July 13, 1865, the same Congregation of the Holy Office issued another rescript, treating the matter at greater length. It was occasioned by a question proposed by the Archbishops of Baltimore, New York and Cincinnati and by the Bishops of Albany, Brooklyn, Buffalo, Burlington, Hartford, Newark and Portland. The decree of August 6, 1846 was repeated, and the Congregation declared that if any further difficulties came up, they were

[50] Pollard, *The Secret Societies of Ireland*, p. 57.

[51] *Collectanea, S. C. P. F.*, II, p. 33, No. 1350, nota 2.

[52] *C. I. C. Fontes*, IV, p. 177, No. 899.

to be referred to the Holy See for settlement. And since it was asserted in certain newspapers, especially in the *Connaught Patriot,* that the Holy See had declared the Fenians should not be disquieted, this falsehood was denied.[53]

It would surely seem from the above decree that the Fenians were certainly condemned, yet, after the promulgation of the constitution " Apostolicae Sedis ", the Holy See found it necessary to declare that the Fenians were comprehended among the societies forbidden and condemned by the Pontifical constitutions, and especially did they come under the censure of the constitution " Apostolicae Sedis ", against *nomen dantes, fautores* and *occultos coriphaeos ac duces non denunciantes.*[54] This decree was dated January 12, 1870, and it put an end forever to the controversy about the Fenians.[55]

ARTICLE II.   THE CONDEMNATION OF SECRET SOCIETIES

In the year 1846, January 26, Bishop Kenrick, then of Philadelphia, and later Archbishop of Baltimore, addressed a letter to the Prefect of the Sacred Congregation of the Propaganda, in which he asked whether those societies should be considered forbidden, which, although they denied that they machinated against either Church or state, nevertheless bound themselves by oath, or other solemn engagement to secrecy.[1] After three months, when no answer was forthcoming, even though in the Bishop's mind the question was of the greatest importance, he again wrote the Holy See to the same effect.[2]

---

[53] *C. I. C. Fontes,* IV, p. 261, No. 986.

[54] *C. I. C. Fontes,* III, p. 27, No. 552.

[55] *C. I. C. Fontes,* IV, pp. 316-317, No. 1012.

[1] Conc. Plen. Balt. II, *Acta et Decreta,* appendix xxviii.

[2] Conc. Plen. Balt. II, *Acta et Decreta,* appendix xxviii.

Meanwhile the Holy Office, August 5, 1846, declared in a rescript that the occult societies spoken of in the Pontifical Constitutions were to be understood as all those that proposed for themselves anything against Church or state.[3] The purpose of this decree was to show that those occult societies that conspired against either the Church or state were the occult societies spoken of in the Pontifical Constitutions.[4] The societies to which Bishop Kenrick referred professed that they neither did nor meditated anything against either Church or state: hence it could be legitimately concluded that they were not condemned.

Two years after the last letter of Bishop Kenrick, the Holy Office answered by declaring that the societies spoken of by him were comprehended in the Pontifical Constitutions, " comprehendi in Pontificiis Constitutionibus ". Cardinal Frasconi in a letter accompanying the rescript of the Holy Office explained to the Bishop the meaning of the response, and how the secrecy and occultness with which these societies were enshrouded were the principal reason of their condemnation. This also was to be the norm for deciding in the future, when the occasion presented itself.[5] This response, it is readily seen, obscured the issue to no little extent.

It was certain, then, that these societies were condemned, but it was by no means certain that their members were under censure. It is true that the Holy Office, August 5, 1846, said that the occult societies spoken of in the Pontifical Constitutions were to be understood as those societies conspiring against Church or state, and that Bishop Kenrick had been answered that merely secret societies were comprehended in the Pontifical Constitutions: still it is not true that the re-

---

[3] *Collectanea S. C. P. F.,* II, p. 7, No. 1320.

[4] Cf. *Acta Sanctae Sedis,* I, pp. 290, *seq.*

[5] Conc. Plen. Balt. II, *Acta et Decreta,* appendix xxviii: cf. also Pennacchi, *Com. in Con. Apos. Sed.,* I, p. 615.

sponse of August 5, 1846, defined what the Holy See meant by secret, occult, or clandestine societies, and that " comprehendi in Pontificiis Constitutionibus " meant that the societies in question were under censure.   As the editor of the *Acta Sanctae Sedis* points out, the decree of August 5, 1846 was intended to show that the " vel " of the phrase " contra Ecclesiam vel rempublicam " was disjunctive, since it was claimed by the Fenians and their followers that they were not condemned and excommunicated by the Apostolic Bulls, particularly " Quo Graviora ", against all anti-social societies, because they did not machinate against the Church, but only against the Protestant English Government of Ireland, which was to them unjust, and not a " potestas legitima ".[6]   Moreover a society could be comprehended in the Pontifical Constitutions without being at the same time excommunicated, for in the constitution " Quo Graviora " other than the anti-social societies were mentioned, for example, the secret societies that were springing up at the universities, and the excommunication was directed only against societies " occultas omnes tam quae nunc sunt, tam quae fortasse erumpent, et quae superius commemoravimus, quocumque nomine appellentur ".   What societies were meant here we learn from the preceding paragraph, namely, those societies which were endeavoring to overturn legitimate governments, and to wipe out the Church.[7]

The reason of the excommunication was the anti-social activities of the censured societies; the reason for the condemnation of merely secret societies was, according to the Cardinal Prefect of the Propaganda, the secrecy and occultness in which they were enveloped.   The oath of secrecy usually exacted by the anti-social societies, the Holy See

[6] *Acta Sanctae Sedis,* I, p. 290, seq.

[7] Cf. Const. "Quo Graviora", March 13, 1825, *C. I. C. Fontes,* II, p. 733, No. 481, parapraphs 7, 10, 11, & 12.

declared, had nothing at all to do with their excommunication.[8]

When Pope Pius IX promulgated the constitution " Apostolicae Sedis ", he seemed to clear up all doubts concerning these merely secret societies.[9] Moreover the Holy Office, February 1, 1871, in an instruction to the Vicar Apostolic of Mysore, now a suffragan see of the Province of Pondicherry, in answer to a question concerning the Odd Fellows, declared that society illicit, but said nothing about excommunication.[10] Hence, using the reflex principles of the Regulae Iuris, XV and XLIX, the conclusion was that the Odd Fellows were not under censure.

There were, however, some theologians who still maintained that these societies were nevertheless under censure.[11] It is said that they took their stand upon the principle that those societies which exacted from their members absolute secrecy and blind obedience established thereby a strong suspicion that they were plotting against religious, or civil authority, which presumption seems to have been taken as proof of the fact.[12]

The Holy Office, May 10, 1884, introduced a definite norm by which societies condemned under censure could be distinguished, in general, from societies condemned without censure. This was given in an Instruction addressed to the Episcopate on the *modus agendi* to be followed with regard to the Masons and the members of other societies. The Sacred Congregation declared that the societies which fell

---

[8] *Acta Sanctae Sedis,* I. p. 292.

[9] *C. I. C. Fontes,* III, p. 27, No. 552, c. II, n. 4.

[10] *C. I. C. Fontes,* IV, p. 332, No. 1014, paragraph 4.

[11] Cf. Konings, Theo. Mor. II, No. 1721: Marc, *Inst. Mor. Alphonsianae,* No. 133,: Rohling, *Medulla Theo. Mor.,* p. 436.

[12] *Eccl. Review,* I, p. 183.

under the censure of Part II, N. 4. of the Constitution " Apostolicae Sedis " were the Freemasons, and other socie- ties " eiusdem generis . . . quaeque contra Ecclesiam vel legitimas potestates machinantur, sive id clam, sive palam fecerint, sive exigerint sive non a suis asseclis secreti servandi iuramentum ". Besides these excommunicated societies, there were others that were forbidden also, " atque sub gravis culpae reatu ", and societies that demanded an oath of secrecy or of blind obedience were especially numbered among the latter.[13]

The question finally resulted in the nominal condemnation of four merely secret societies, of the Independent Order of Good Templars, August 3, 1893,[14] and of the Odd Fellows, the Knights of Pythias, and the Sons of Temperance, August 20, 1894.[15]

ARTICLE III.   CONDEMNATION OF BIBLE SOCIETIES

The Council of Trent in the decree " De Editione et Usu Sacrorum Librorum " declared that the Vulgate was the authentic version of the Sacred Scriptures to be used for all public readings, sermons, disputations and expositions; that all new editions of the Bible were to be the Vulgate published as carefully as possible; that no one could publish, or have published books " de rebus divinis " [1] without the name of the author; and that no one could sell such books, or even keep them in his possession unless first examined and ap-

[13] *C. I. C. Fontes,* IV, p. 415, No. 1085.

[14] *C. I. C. Fontes,* IV, p. 482, No. 1167.

[15] *C. I. C. Fontes,* IV, p. 484, No. 1171.

[1] The S. C. Holy Office, December 22, 1880, declared the term "de rebus divinis" "restringendum esse ad libros sacrarum scripturarum, nec non earumdem adnotationes et commentarios, minime vero extendendum ad libros quoscumque de rebus sacris in genere, id est ad religionem pertinentibus tractantes". *A. S. S.,* vol. XXVIII, p. 64.

proved by the Ordinary under pain of the excommunication and fine imposed by the Fifth Lateran Council, Session X, May 4, 1515.[2]

Towards the end of the council the censorship of books was discussed resulting in the " Index Tridentinus " published in 1564 along with the brief " Dominici Gregis " of Pius IV.[3] Besides the catalogue of forbidden books, ten general rules were decreed, numbers three and four of which have special reference to the Sacred Scriptures. According to these, the Bible done into the vernacular was to be permitted only to those whom the reading of the Sacred Text in the *vernacular would not harm,* but increase in faith and piety.[4]

---

[2] *Acta et Decreta Sacrosancti Oecumenici Concilii Tridentini,* Sessio IV, " de Editione et Usu Sacrorum Librorum "; reference to the Fifth Council of the Lateran in Mansi, vol. 32, col. 912.

[3] *C. I. C. Fontes,* I, p. 186, No. 105.

[4] *Index Librorum Prohibitorum,* ed. novissima, Romae, 1877. " Versiones scriptorum etiam ecclesiasticorum, quae hactenus editae sunt a damnatis auctoribus, modo nihil contra sanam doctrinam contineant, permittuntur. Librorum autem veteris testamenti versiones, viris, tantum doctis et piis judicio episcopi concedi poterunt; modo hujusmodi versiones tanquam elucidationibus vulgatae editionis, ad intelligendam sacram scripturam, non autem tanquam sano textu utantur. Versiones, vero, novi testamenti, ab auctoribus primae classis (i. e., of the Index, viz., ' Libri ab haereticis scripti vel editi, aut ad eos sive ad infideles pertinentes ') hujus indicis factae nemini concedantur; quia utilitatis parum, periculi vero plurimum lectoribus ex earum lectione manare solet. Si quae vero annotationes cum hujusmodi quae permittuntur versionibus, vel cum vulgata editione circumferuntur, expunctis locis suspectis a facultate theologica universitatis catholicae, aut inquisitione generali, permitti eisdem poterunt, quibus et versiones. Quibus conditionibus totum volumen biblorum quod vulgo biblia Vatabili dicitur, aut partes eius concedi viris piis et doctis poterunt. Ex bibliis vero Isidori Clarii brixani prologus et prolegomena praecidantur; eius vero textum, nemo textum vulgatae editiones esse existimet.

" Cum experimento manifestum sit, si sacra biblia vulgari lingua passim sine discrimine permittantur, plus inde ob hominum temeritatem,

The Sacred Congregation of the Index, instituted by St. Pius V, in the year 1571, as the " Sacra Congregatio de Reformando Indice et Corrigendis Libris ",[5] decreed, June 17, 1757 that vernacular editions of the Sacred Scriptures could not be permitted " nisi quae fuerint ab Apostolica Sede approbatae et editae cum adnotationibus desumptis ex Sanctis Ecclesiae Patribus, vel doctis catholicisque viris ".[6] As it stood the legislation concerning the Bible in the vernacular prohibited unauthorized editions to be either published, read, or possessed, and a translation into the vernacular to be authorized other than by the Holy See had to be annotated from approved authors.

Bible Societies, by the beginning of the nineteenth century, were getting under way, especially the British and Foreign Bible Society, " the Mother of them all ". Its nefarious work was being carried on in Poland and Russia, in the first quarter of the nineteenth century. Pius VII, therefore wrote the Archbishop of Gnesen a brief, headed " Postremus Litteris " against them. This was the first formal notice taken by the Holy See of Bible Societies, and

detrimenti, quam utilitatis oriri, hac in parte judicio episcopi aut inquisitoris stetur; ut cum consilio parochi, vel confessarii, biblorum a catholicis auctoribus versorum lectionem in vulgari lingua eis concedere possint, quos intellexerint ex hujusmodi lectione non damnum, sed fidei atque pietatis augmentum capere posse; quam facultatem in scriptis habeant. Qui autem absque tali facultate ea legere seu habere praesumpserit, nisi prius bibliis ordinario redditis, peccatorum absolutionem precipere non possit. Bibliopolae vero qui praedictam facultatem non habenti biblia idiomate vulgari conscripta vendiderint, vel alio quovis modo concesserint, librorum praetium in usus pios ab episcopo convertendum amittant, aliisque poenis pro delicti qualitate eiusdem episcopi arbitrio subiaceant. Regulares vero nonnisi facultate a praelatis suis habita, ea legere, aut emere possint ". *Acta et Decreta Oecumenici Concilii Tridentini*, Regulae Indicis Decem, p. 338 to p. 345.

[5] Ojette, " Roman Congregations," *Cath. Ency.*, XIII, p. 143.

[6] *C. I. C. Fontes*, II, p. 801, No. 502, footnote 5.

was occasioned by the Archbishop's denunciation of their work to the Holy See, especially of the abuses they were perpetrating in Poland. The Pontiff exhorted the Archbishop to remind the faithful of his Archdiocese of the " Regulae Indicis " of the Council of Trent, and he asked that a copy of the Polish Bible prepared by Jacobus Wichius, under Bible Society auspices and published by it, be sent to Rome together with the Archbishop's opinion of the work, in order that the proper pronouncement might be given.[7]

That same year, September 4, the Holy Father addresses another letter, this time to the Archbishop of Mihiloff in Russia, in which, after lamenting the violation of the law of the Church in the matter of the use and publication of the Sacred Scriptures, as well as their translation, he pointed out that the good obtained by permitting their translation into the vernacular, " without note or comment ", as is the boast of Bible Societies, would be far out-weighed by the detriment which such versions would cause to souls. He recalled how Trent had commanded that the Church receive only the Vulgate,[8] " porro Romana Ecclesia solam vulgatam editione ex notissimo Tridentini Concilii praescripto suscipiens ", etc., for the Bible Societies rejected the Canon of the Scriptures defined by Trent, publishing only the *Proto-Canonical* Books. He showed how that Council permitted versions in other languages only when properly annotated.[9]

August 3, 1816, the Sacred Congregation of the Propaganda in a letter to the Vicars Apostolic of Persia, Armenia, and several other Oriental countries, denounced the work of the colporteurs, or Bible-hawkers, among the natives of those lands. It was followed the next year, June 23, 1817,

[7] De Martinis, *Jus Pontificium*, Pars. I, vol. IV, lxi, p. 544.

[8] *Acta et Decreta S. O. Concilii Tridentini*, Sessio IV, De Editione et Usu Sacrorum Librorum.

[9] Denzinger-Bannwart, *Enchiridion Symbolorum*, etc. No. 1603.

by a decree of the Sacred Congregation of the Index pro-
hibiting a book entitled *Historia Succincta delle Operationi
della Compagnia Biblia Brittanica e Straniere, coll 'indice
delle matterie concernenti la medesima,* published at Naples
in 1817.　All versions of the Bible in the vernacular were
also prohibited by this decree, unless they were approved by
the Holy See, or edited with annotations taken from the
Fathers, or from learned Catholic writers according to the
prescription of the Index, June 17, 1757, given *supra*.[10]

In the Encyclical " Ubi Primum ", written on his accession
to the Sovereign Pontificate, Leo XII mentioned the Bible
Societies *inter cetera.*　He deplored that they were
speading the Sacred Scriptures all over the world, devoid
of the proper footnotes, thereby violating the decrees of the
Council of Trent.　He added that he was not ignorant concerning " societatem quamdam vulgo biblicam . . . quae
spretis SS. PP. traditionibus et contra notissimum Tridentini
Concilii decretum, in id collatis viribus et modis omnibus
intendit ut in vulgares linguas nationum omnium vertantur,
vel potius pervertantur ".　Finally, recounting the letters of
His predecessor, Pius VII, to the Metropolitans of Gnesen
and Mihiloff, he encouraged the Bishops to guard their flocks
against the cunning of the Bible sectaries, as well as to in-
struct them in the " Regulae Indicis ".　This was dated May
5, 1824.[11]

Pius VIII, May 21, 1829, also in the encyclical written on
the occasion of his elevation to the See of Peter, by name
" Traditi ", spoke against Bible Societies, and how they translated the Bible into all languages, contorting the Holy Word
to suit their private judgment, and disregarding the laws of
the Church.[12]

[10] *C. I. C. Fontes,* II, p. 800, " 502 ", footnote 6.

[11] *Bullarii Romani Continuatio,* XIII, p. 57.

[12] *Bull. Rom. Continuatio,* XIV, p. 23.

The whole movement of the Church against Bible Societies culminated in the Encyclical Letter " Inter Praecipuas " of Gregory XVI, May 5, 1844.[13]   These societies had been calumniating the Holy See, as they do even today, " quasi a pluribus jam saeculis fidelem populum a Sacrarum Scripturarum cognitione arcere conetur ".[14]   They had forgotten the efforts that had been made that the Catholic people might learn more and more the Word of God, both written, and, what is equally important, Tradition.   The Lutherans and Calvinists had left nothing undone to deceive the faithful by their perverse explanations of the Holy Writ, publishing through the Bible Societies hundreds of copies of their perverted Bibles by means of the newly invented typography. Gregory recounted, then, the many warnings of His Predecessors, stating that he himself had not failed to be solicitous towards the same end, having seen to it that the " Regulae " governing the translation of the Sacred Writ were again brought to the notice of the faithful.[15]

The Holy Father, continuing, then took up the Christian Alliance, *Foedus Christianum,* founded June 1, 1843, in

[13] *C. I. C. Fontes,* II, p. 797, No. 502.

[14] *C. I. C. Fontes,* II, p. 797, No. 502, paragraph 3.

[15] *C. I. C. Fontes,* II, p. 801, footnote 5.   " Cum ad S. Congregationem certo relatum fuerit sacratissimos Biblorum libros vulgari sermone nonnullis in locis typis edi quin saluberrimae de re leges serventur; cumque inde pertimescendum sit ne, quae hominum nequam hisce praesertim temporibus conspiratio est, errores sanctiori divini eloquii apparatu obvoluti perperam insinuentur, censuit eadem S. Congregatio revocanda iterum esse in omnium memoriam, quae alias decreta sunt; vernaculas nimium Bibliorum versiones non esse permittendas, nisi quae fuerint ab apostolica Sede approbatae aut editae cum adnotationibus desumptis ex SS. Ecclesiae Patribus, vel ex doctis Catholicisque viris (ex decreto Sacrae Congregationis Indicis, 17 Junii, 1757, in addit. ad reg. Ind.), iis praeterea omnino insistendum quae per regulam quartam Indicis et deinceps ex mandato s. m. Clementis VIII, in eam causam praestituta fuerint."

New York, for the purpose of injecting religious indiffer-ence, or, as they would have had it, religious liberty among the Catholic Italians, and even among those in Rome itself.[16]

Pope Gregory, therefore, condemned all Bible Societies, and reproved and condemned *nominatim* the Christian Alliance, and all its branches, (et alia eiusdem generis sodali-tia, si quae jam ei accesserint, aut in posterum accedent), adding " Hinc notum sit omnibus gravissimi coram Deo et Ecclesia criminis reos fore illos omnes, qui alicui earumdem societatum dare nomen, aut operam suam commodare seu quomodocumque favere praesumpserint ". He confirmed and renewed all the above mentioned prescriptions of the Holy See concerning the editing, publishing, reading and possessing of the Sacred Scriptures translated into the ver-nacular, desiring that they be strictly obeyed.[17] And he concluded by exhorting the Bishops to announce and explain to their flock the Papal pronouncement against Bible Socie-ties and the *Foedus Christianum.*

Finally, Pius IX, in his initial Encyclical " Qui Pluribus " having described the Bible Societies as *Vaferrimae Biblicae Societates,* followed the example of his predecessors, especi-ally Gregory XVI, and condemned again all Bible Societies.[18]

ARTICLE IV. THE CONDEMNATION OF CREMATION SOCIETIES

Cremation is against the traditions of the religions of both the Old and the New Testaments. There are many and manifest examples in Scripture of how the Jews scrupul-

[16] *C. I. C. Fontes,* II, No. 502. Text as follows:—" Quorum commune consilium sit ut religiosam libertatem, seu potius versanum indifferentiae super religione studium Romanis Italisque ceteris infundant ".

[17] *C. I. C. Fontes,* II, No. 502, paragraph 11.

[18] *C. I. C. Fontes,* II, No. 504, para. 5. Text as follows: " Quas so-cietates Suorum Decessorum Exempla aemulans recol. men. Gregorius XVI, in cuius locum meritis licet imparibus suffecti sumus, suis Apostolicis Litteris reprobavit, Nos pariter damnatas esse volumus ".

ously saw to it that their sacred dead were buried, and not
burnt, as was the practice of the Gentiles.[1]   The text " dust
thou art, and unto dust thou shalt return " was repeatedly
quoted by the Rabbis as their reason for preferring inhumation,[2] and even Tacitus records of the Jews that they were
wont to bury, rather than burn their dead.[3]

What was the early Christian sentiment in the matter is
well expressed in the words of Minutius Felix in his
Octavius:—" Nec ut creditis ullum damnum sepulturae time-
mus, sed veterem et meliorem consuetudinem inhumandi fre-
quentamus ".[4]   From the centuries of the Apostolic Age to
the beginning of the Medieval Period, inhumation, attended
by the touching ritual of Catholic Sepulture, was the universal practice of the Christian world.

In the thirteenth century, following the Crusades, it became a practice that the praecordia of those who died far
from home were removed, and their bodies boiled to separate
the flesh from the bones, in order to facilitate their transfer
to their native lands.   This was certainly against the feeling
of the greater majority of the faithful.   To put an end to
this detestable abuse Pope Boniface VIII issued a decree
forbidding its practice, excommunicating all who performed
it, and denying ecclesiastical sepulture to all bodies so im-
piously and cruelly mutilated.[5]   This is the only legislation
passed during the middle ages that in any way refers to cremation.

In the last century, however, cremation was again intro-

---

[1] Gen. 23 : 3, 6, 13-19; Tob., 4 : 3, 5; II Kings 9 : 9, 10; Jer. 8 : 1, 2;
II Macc. 4 : 7, 9, 11.

[2] Cf. *Eccl. Review*, IV, p. 24.

[3] *Hist.*, V, 5.

[4] Migne, *Pat. Lat.*, III, col. 347.

[5] C. 1, de sep., III, 6, in *Extravag. Com.*

duced into the Christian world, and soon became the sign of religious indifference, the denial of the resurrection of the body, and of disbelief in the existence of a supreme Being. It was openly espoused by Freemasonry, at Naples, in 1869,[6] and also became a sign of adherence to the principles of that craft.[7] Cremation interferes with the rites and ceremonies attendant on inhumation, weakens the reverence for the dead that is based, not on mere sentiment, but upon facts of faith, and by no means outweighs, with its supposed hygienic advantages, the religious feelings aroused by the old custom of burying the dead. And its advocates are, in almost every case, either avowed atheists, or professed Freemasons.[8]

It is but natural that we should reverence that which was but a short time before the temple of life and the tabernacle of the Holy Ghost. Mankind holds in the greatest abhorrence the shameless ghoul who robs the coffins and mutilates the bodies of the dead. Necessity alone sanctions a disregarding of this instinct, and the isolated instance of the dissecting-room must be considered *pari passu* with the amputation of a living member, licit only when the life and the health of the whole body, or of the commonweal, demands it.[9] There is no such necessity for the practice of cremation. It has been demonstrated that even where there is but a small quantity of oxygen in a grave, a body will decompose naturally and odorlessly, which, if left in the open air, would quickly corrupt, and emit an offensive stench. The plea that inhumation contaminates and pollutes rain-water, and hence the supply of drinking water of the earth, has been shown by several scientists to be groundless. Only one third of

---

[6] Augustine, *Commentary*, VI, p. 101.

[7] Cf. *S. C. S. Off.*, 19 Maii, 1886, *C. I. C. Fontes*, IV, p. 428, No. 1100.

[8] *Ecc. Review*, IV, pp. 18-20.

[9] Cf. *Eccl. Review*, IV, p. 21; also Genicot, *Theo. Mor. Inst.*, ed. 1897, II, p. 805.

the annual rainfall ever penetrates the earth, and this third which does actually penetrate cannot become infectious, because its passage through the ground will entirely filter it. Indeed water from a city sewer has been passed for many months through six and a half feet of sand, and always came out at the bottom pure, clean and drinkable.[10]

Now it happened that in India where the practice of cremation of the dead is prehistoric, the lawfulness of its practice by Christians, even when it was stripped of all pagan customs, was called into doubt. A case was sent by the Vicar Apostolic of Vizagapatam, Msgr. Tissot, to the Holy See for solution. Two neophytes had been cremated. Their relatives had done this because it was a caste privilege. The prelate added that his priests were wont to baptize a pagan who sought baptism at the moment of death, and did not bother to inquire whether he would be cremated or buried. What was to be done in the matter? In response the Holy Office answered that the prelate should not approve of cremation, but that baptism should always be conferred, and that the people should be properly instructed concerning cremation.[11]

Regarding the above decision, the editor of the *Ecclesiastical Review* remarked that it was exceptional, and that in it might be found the reason why the Holy See does not always add a definite censure to a general injunction against a threatening abuse: the custom was centuries-old in India, and the caste privileges are part and parcel of the Indian character. Among us, to tolerate cremation would cause scandal, while in India to forbid it would do so.[12] This was, it is true, a toleration of cremation, but only for India, and

---

[10] Devlin, " Cremation ", *Cath. Ency.*, IV, p. 483.

[11] *S. C. S. Off.*, Jan. 1888, *C. I. C. Fontes*, IV, p. 433, No. 1108.

[12] *Eccl. Review*, X, pp. 231-232.

only under the circumstances noted. However, it was also a non-approbation of the practice, for Msgr. Tissot was warned, " cremationem approbare non debes ".

Two years later, the Holy Office formally condemned cremation societies. It seems that many Bishops from all parts of the world had been petitioning the Holy See to make some definite pronouncement in the issue. To settle the matter, in Sacred Congregation, May 19, 1886, declared it was illicit to join cremation societies, and that those who did so, if the society were affiliated with Masonry, incurred the same penalties as the members of that sect. It was also declared illicit to command that one's own, or another's body, be cremated.[13]

Later that same year, December 15, the Holy Office again decreed that those who, not of their own free will, but at the will of others, were to be cremated, might receive the rites and suffrages of the Church, at home and in church, but not on the way to, or at, the crematory, under the condition that scandal be removed. How scandal was to be removed was demonstrated by the decree : it was to be made known that the corpse was cremated, not at the command of the deceased, but of another. Those who had commanded that their bodies be cremated, and had persevered in this choice until death, were to be denied ecclesiastical sepulture according to the prescription of the Roman Ritual.[14]

Some years later, the Bishop of Friburg asked the Holy Office whether those Catholics who, although not Masons, nor influenced by Masonic principles, but for other reasons, had commanded that their bodies be cremated, could receive the last sacraments, if they refused to retract their desire : whether those who, of their own accord, were to be cremated, could have Mass offered publicly, or privately, and whether

---

[13] *C. I. C. Fontes,* IV, p. 428, No. 1100.
[14] *Rituale Romanum,* tit. VI, c. ii, n. 8.

it were licit to accept mass-foundations for that purpose; whether it were ever allowed to cooperate in cremation, either by counsel, or command, or because of necessity, or for fear of grave loss; and whether it were lawful to admit to the sacraments those who could not, or said they could not, desist from such cooperation. The answer was that those who commanded that their bodies be cremated were to be warned to retract their command: if they refused to do so, they were to be denied the sacraments. However, the principles of moral theology were to be followed in deciding whether or not the warning should be made. Mass could not be publicly offered for those who had commanded cremation, but it could be, privately. It was never permissible to coöperate formally, either by command or counsel, in cremation: material coöperation, the mere aiding in the physical act, could be tolerated on condition that; 1. Cremation was not looked upon as a distinctive sign of Freemasonry; 2. That there was nothing in it which of itself directly and solely expressed reprobation of Catholic teaching, and the approbation of the sect; 3. If it were not certainly clear that the officials and others, e. g., laborers, had been assigned or ordered to take part in cremation in contempt of the Catholic religion. And whereas, under the above restrictions, coöperators were always to be left in good faith, they were, however, to be warned not to intend coöperation in cremation.[15]

There were several other decrees concerning cremation after the year 1892, for example, that of the Holy Office, August 3, 1897, which dealt with the cremation of amputated corporeal members, and that of the same congregation, June 19, 1921.[16] These do not, however, deal directly with cremation societies, and hence are of little interest here.

[15] *S. C. S. Off.*, 27 Julii, 1892, *C. I. C. Fontes,* IV, p. 478, No. 1157.
[16] *C. I. C. Fontes,* IV, pp. 494, No. 1189.

ARTICLE V. THE CONDEMNATION OF THEOSOPHICAL
SOCIETIES

The history of the condemnation of Theosophical Societies
is rather brief.   In a plenary meeting of the Sacred Congregation of the Holy Office, June 16, 1919, a question was proposed, whether the teachings of theosophy were in accord
with Catholic faith, and whether it were lawful to join
theosophical societies, and read theosophical literature, books,
periodicals, newspapers and other writings.   The decision
was " Negative in omnibus ".   It is, therefore, forbidden to
join theosophical societies, but, although these societies were
condemned, no mention of censure was in the rescript.[1]

ARTICLE VI.   THE SECOND AND THIRD PLENARY COUNCILS
OF BALTIMORE AND CONDEMNED SOCIETIES

In Title XII of the Acts and Decrees of the Second
Plenary Council of Baltimore, the Fathers reviewed the
condemnations of the Masons, Carbonari and similar sects,
pronounced by Clement XII, Benedict XIV, Pius VII, Leo
XII, Pius VIII, and Pius IX, then gloriously reigning, and
they incorporated into the Acts of the Council the decree of
the Fourth Provincial Council of Baltimore, convened by
Archbishop Eccleston, May 16, 1840:—

Propter gravissimas rationes vetuerunt SS. Pontifices ne
fideles secretas societates quovis nomine nuncupatas ineant,
jurejurando sese adstringentes ad arcana servanda. Nam
foedera hujusmodi clanculum inita, mali suspicionem et periculum prae se ferunt, et jusjurandum temere adhibetur.
Idcirco monemus Sacerdotes omnes neminem posse absolutione
sacramentali donari, nisi ab hujusmodi societatibus prorsus re-
cedat. Hortamur autem, et in Domino absecremus fideles
omnes ut occulta illa foedera omnino declinent, mente revol-
ventes se Christi membra esse, et Ecclesiae quae mater nostra

[1] *Acta Apostolicae Sedis*, XI, p. 317.

est mandatis teneri, eosque ut filios lucis debere ambulare, juxta sanctissima illa documenta quae Christus Dominus tradidit.[1]

The letter of Bishop Kenrick to the Prefect of the Propaganda and its answer by the Holy Office were given, and the well known controversy whether or not Labor Unions were to be considered condemned societies was taken up. After stating the reasons brought forth by Benedict XIV as " inter gravissimas praefatae prohibitionis et damnationis causas ", i. e., of the condemnation of the Masons,[2] and the response of the Holy Office, of August 26, 1846, which, unless taken in its entire context and history, is so easily misunderstood,[3] the Fathers decided that Labor Unions were not condei ined societies.

The Council very wisely prohibited the nominal condemnation of any society by any cleric, no matter what his dignity or office, " nisi certo et praeter omne dubium constet (eam) ex illis esse, quae Constitutionibus Pontificiis comprehenduntur ", and ordered that recourse be had to the Holy See as often as necessary, " omnibus adamussim expositis adiunctis ".[4] Finally, the faithful were warned and exhorted to avoid all condemned societies, and even those questionable societies that did not seem to be included in the strict censures of the Church.[5]

The Third Plenary Council of Baltimore commented, in

---

[1] *Conc. Prov. Balt. Habita 1829-1840*, p. 172, VII.

[2] Cf. Const. "Providas", May 18, 1751, *C. I. C. Fontes*, II, p. 315, No. 412.

[3] Cf. *Acta Sanctae Sedis*, I, p. 290.

[4] Cf. *Acta Sanctae Sedis*, I, p. 290, rescript of the Holy Office, August 5, 1846.

[5] Cf. *Conc. Plen. Balt.* II, Acta et Decreta, tit. XII, cap. unic., Nos. 511-523.

the first place, on the many ways the hostility of Free-masonry to the Church was demonstrated, and commanded that the Pontifical decrees against these societies be pro-claimed and executed. That there were societies other than the Freemasons and Carbonari, and differing from them "nomine, ritu, forma, origine", which also came under the declarations of the Holy See, since they were *eiusdem generis* as the societies condemned nominally and under cen-sure, the norms by which a society could be distinguished as condemned, or not condemned, and the justice of the condem-nation, were also shown. The Fathers also pointed certain *ipso facto* censures the members of a society could incur, even though it were not anti-social, " si presbyterum proprio marte sibi vindicet aliumve ministrum cultus, qui rituali ac caeremoniis propriis pro suo libitu utatur ", namely those censures against heretics, and schismatics of Part I, number 1 of the Constitution " Apostolicae Sedis ".[6] The Council ex-plained, however, that to incur this censure the society must have these priests, or ministers, and its rites and ceremonies, " non quomodolibet, nec sicuti aliquando apud nostrates fit cum preces quaedam in civium conventibus recitantur, sed eo modo quo ipsa societas, pravo fine proposito, secta schis-matica aut haeretica evadit ". But when a society has gone so far that it has become a schismatic or heretical sect, it would seem to be no longer a mere society, but rather a non-Catholic religion.

The censure contained in the Constitution " Apostolicae Sedis " against the Masons, Carbonari, and other sects *eiusdem generis* was repeated by the Fathers who de-clared: " Has igitur censuras . . . nullo modo aut tacendas aut dissimulandas esse; sed econtra manifeste promulgandas atque in reos urgendas." The conclusion of the Second

[6] Const. "Apostolicae Sedis", 12 Octobris, 1869, *C. I. C. Fontes*, III, p. 25, No. 552.

Plenary Council that Labor Unions were not condemned was upheld, and the Archbishops of the country were constituted a commission to judge whether or not a society were condemned, and if condemned, whether or not those who joined it were excommunicated. A provision was attached to this appointment, that if the Archbishops could not unanimously agree, the whole affair was to be referred to the Holy See. This closed the article.[7]

[7] *Conc. Plen. Balt.* III, Acta et Decreta, tit. VIII, cap. iii, art. I, Nos. 244-255.

CHAPTER III

THE FAITHFUL AND SOCIETIES, APPROVED AND CONDEMNED

CANON 684. GENERAL INTRODUCTORY CANON

FIDELES LAUDE DIGNI SUNT, QUI SUA DENT NOMINA ASSOCIA-
TIONIBUS AB ECCLESIA ERECTIS VEL SALTEM COMMENDATIS:
CAVEANT AUTEM AB ASSOCIATIONIBUS SECRETIS, DAMNATIS,
SEDITIOSIS, SUSPECTIS, AUT QUAE STUDEANT SESE A LEGITIMA
ECCLESIAE VIGILANTIA SUBDUCERE.

MAN, philosophers tell us, is a social animal, and hence, of
his very nature, has a propensity to associate himself with
other men for company, mutual aid, and the like. He is
greatly benefitted by this association with other men, and it
is by no means the intention of the Church, the kindest of
mothers, to deny him the fulfillment of this natural instinct.
It is her duty, and also her right to keep a vigilant eye over
the associations her children make, the societies they join,
and to approve of them or condemn them as circumstances
dictate. The Church, therefore, in this first canon of the
tract on Condemned Societies commends those of her children who join societies that she has either erected, or, at
least, approved, and she warns them against joining societies
which may lead them into sin, or cause them to lose their
immortal souls.[1]

The history of the second part of this canon has already
been seen, and that of the first can be quickly told. Leo

---

[1] Cf. Prümmer, *Manuale Iuris Canonici*, p. 349, No. 269; Vermeersch-
Creusen, *Epitome Iuris Canonici*, I, p. 467, No. 784.

44

XIII never tired of exhorting the faithful to join pious associations, and his antidote for the poison of Freemasonry was the Third Order of St. Francis for which he had a special fondness.[2]

The faithful who join societies either erected or approved by the Church are commended, and thus, indirectly, these societies are recommended to the faithful. Examples of these societies are the Third Orders Secular, the Confraternities, and Pious Unions,[3] the Conferences of St. Vincent de Paul, the Misericordes, the Ladies of Charity, the Knights of Columbus, and the Catholic Students' Mission Crusade.

The faithful are on the contrary to avoid secret, condemned, seditious, and suspected societies, and those that seek to escape the vigilance of the Church.

Augustine says that by " secret societies " is meant " principally the Freemasons." [4] It really seems that much more is meant by the term than merely the Freemasons. Secret Societies are those whose members are bound to secrecy concerning their order, as Vermeersch has it:—" hae enim generali reprobatione ab Ecclesia notantur, saltem quando a sodalibus iusiurandum secreti erga omnes (etiam superiores ecclesiasticos) exigunt, et omnimodam obedientiam occultis ducibus ".[5] He refers for proof of his opinion to the Instruction of the Holy Office, May 10, 1884.[6]

The term " condemned societies " is to be interpreted here as referring to those which the Church has forbidden her

---

[2] Cf. "Misericors Dei Filius ", May 30, 1883, *C. I. C. Fontes,* III, p. 208, No. 588; "Auspicatio", Sept. 17, 1882, *Leonis XIII Acta,* III, p. 142; "Humanum Genus ", April 20, 1884, *C. I. C. Fontes,* III, p. 221, No. 591.

[3] Canon 700.

[4] Augustine, *Commentary,* III, p. 427.

[5] Vermeersch-Creusen, *Epitome Ius. Can.,* I, p. 468, No. 784.

[6] *C. I. C. Fontes,* IV, p. 415, No. 1085.

members to join, either under censure, or " sub gravis culpae reatu ".[7]   Hence by this term are included Bible Societies, Cremation Societies, Theosophical Societies, Anti-social Societies,[8] the Independent Order of Good Templars, the Odd Fellows, the Sons of Temperance, the Knights of Pythias, and all societies exacting an oath of secrecy, or blind obedience.[9]

Seditious societies are those " quae ad rebellionem tendunt ".[10]   Suspected societies are to be understood in the light of the Instruction of the Holy Office May 10, 1884 :—

Animadvertendum insuper est adesse nonnullas societates, quae licet certo statui nequeat, pertineant necne ad has quas memoravimus, dubiae tamen et periculi plenae sunt, tum ob doctrinas quas profitentur, tum ob agendi rationem quam sequuntur iis, quibus ducibus ipsae coalerunt et reguntur.[11]

Societies that seek to avoid the vigilance of ecclesiastical authorities thereby give cause to a strong suspicion that they are illicit, either in purpose, or in the means they establish to attain their purpose.   The Church as the guardian of faith and morals, and as the judge competent to decide in the court of last appeal, whether or not a human act is licit, or illicit, has a right, as has already been said, to investigate the societies the faithful join.   To shun that investigation indicates that there is something to hide.   Hence, the faithful are warned to avoid these societies, just as they are cautioned against secret, condemned and suspicious societies.

[7] Cf. below, Chapter VII, art. 2.

[8] Cf. Canon 2335.

[9] Regarding female societies affiliated to secret societies of men see Fanning, " Secret Societies ", *Cath. Ency.*, XIV, p. 74, who gives answer no. 15, 352 of the Apostolic Delegation, Washington, on the subject.

[10] Cocchi, *Com. in Cod. Iur. Can.*, II, p. 317, No. 172.

[11] *C. I. C. Fontes*, IV, p. 415, No. 1085.   The societies referred to in this citation are anti-social and secret societies.

This canon and canon 2335, which will be seen at length, below, bring over into the code the previous condemnations of condemned societies. These canons are the Code's condemnation of the five classes outlined in the first chapter, for Anti-Social, Secret, Bible, Cremation and Theosophical societies are all included under either of the terms, secret, condemned, or seditious societies.

CHAPTER IV

PENALTIES INCURRED BY THOSE WHO JOIN ANTI-SOCIAL SOCIETIES

CANON 2335

ARTICLE I. THOSE WHO JOIN ANTI-SOCIAL SOCIETIES INCUR IPSO FACTO EXCOMMUNICATION RESERVED SIMPLY TO THE HOLY SEE.

NOMEN DANTES SECTAE MASSONICAE ALIISVE EIUSDEM GENERIS ASSOCIATIONIBUS QUAE CONTRA ECCLESIAM VEL LEGITIMAS CIVILES POTESTATES MACHINANTUR, CONTRAHUNT IPSO FACTO EXCOMMUCATIONEM SEDI APOSTOLICAE SIMPLICITER RESERVATAM.

THE evolution of this canon has already been seen in the Article on the Condemnation of Anti-Social Societies; it will, therefore, be unnecessary to recount it. There are many changes, however, in the law, necessitated by the passing of time, and the changing of conditions, social and political.[1] The law of the Code is substantially the same as that of " Apostolicae Sedis; " it is, though, abbreviated and amended,[2] and the variations will readily be recognized from the following parallel:—

[1] Cf. Pistocchi, *I Canoni Penali,* p. 100.
[2] Cerato, *Censurae Vigentes,* p. 108, No. 55.

48

The Code	Apostolicae Sedis
Nomen dantes	Nomen dantes
sectae massonicae	sectae Massonicae
. . . .	aut Carbonariae
aliisve	aut aliis
eiusdem generis	eiusdem generis
associationibus	sectis
quae contra Ecclesiam	quae contra Ecclesiam
vel legitimas	vel legitimas
civiles	. . . .
potestates	potestates
. . . .	seu palam, seu clandestine,
machinantur	machinantur;
	necnon iisdem sectis favorem
. . . .	qualemcumque praestantes;
	earumve occultos coriphaeos ac
. . . .	duces non denunciantes, donec
	non denunciaverint
contrahunt ipso facto excommuni-	(Excommunicationi latae sententiae
cationem Sedi Apostolicae sim-	Romano Pontifici simpliciter re-
pliciter reservatam.[3]	servatae subiacere declaramus).[4]

It will be noted that the Carbonari are no longer mentioned; the reason for their omission is, they are no longer in existence.[5] The clauses *favorem praestantes* and *occultos coriphaeos . . . non denunciantes* are also omitted, and therefore supressed, as shall presently be seen.

Those who incur the excommunication of this canon are said to be the *nomen dantes,* which term must be interpreted strictly.[6] It includes " all those who join the Masons or similar societies,[7] who knowingly and willingly enter, or make themselves members of these sects,[8] whether they are

[3] Canon 2335.

[4] *C. I. C. Fontes,* III, p. 27, No. 552.

[5] Kirsch, " Carbonari ", *Cath. Ency.,* III, p. 331.

[6] Canon 2219; 1 & 3.

[7] Ayrinhac, *Penal Legislation,* p. 240, No. 257.

[8] D'Annibale, in *Commentarium in Const.* "Apostolicae Sedis", No. 117; quoted by Cappello, *De Censuris,* ed. 1925, p. 267, No. 296. Ballerini-Palmieri, VII, p. 250, No. 451: 2.

simply and unceremoniously accepted as associates, or initiated with great pomp and ritual.[9] Whether they take an active part in the society, or perhaps never frequent a meeting has no bearing on the question.[10] It is enough to be a *nomen dans* that the one joining know the sect he is about to join is condemned and those who join it excommunicated; he need not know that the society actually wars against the Church, or State, and hence *bona fides* concerning the purposes of the sect does not excuse one from the censure who knows of the condemnation and censure.[11]

Telch is of the opinion that those who favor these sects still incur excommunication.[12] Cerato seems unable to make up his mind about the favorers; he says that the new law prudently omits the *qualemcunque favorem praestantes* and *non denunciantes,* " sive vigeat can. 2209, sive ne latius censura pateat ".[13] In other words the omission is either covered by Canon 2209, or means that the censure is no longer in force. Vermeersch, however, rightly says that the excommunication against them is suppressed by the code,[14] as so also does Ayrinhac.[15] It does not seem possible that the members of the Commission on the Codification did not have the regulations of the constitution " Apostolicae Sedis " before their eyes and minds when framing this canon. Moreover the stricter view is against the principles of the Code. Canon 19 states that laws establishing penalties must be interpreted strictly, and Canon 2219, that penalties can-

[9] Bucceroni, ed. 6a, IV, p. 242, No. 1194.

[10] Blat., *Com. in Tex. Cod. Iur. Can.,* V, p. 225, No. 176.

[11] Cerato, *Censurae Vigentes,* p. 107, No. 55.

[12] *Epitome Theo. Mor.,* p. 198.

[13] *Censurae Vigentes,* p. 107, No. 55.

[14] Vermeersch-Creusen, *Epitome Iur. Can.,* III, p. 277.

[15] *Penal Legislation,* p. 241, No. 257.

not be extended from one case to another, though there is an equal, or even a greater reason. Since, therefore, the Code omits the favorers and those who neglect to denounce the occult leaders, they are no longer excommunicated.[16]

Cerato refers to Canon 2209,—" sive vigeat can. 2209 ".[17] This canon has some place here in conjunction with canon 2231; not so much in regard to *fautores* as to co-operators.[18] This Canon 2209 deals with coöperation; Canon 2231 states that if many coöperated in a crime, even though only one is mentioned in the law, all those coöperators mentioned in paragraphs 1-3 of Canon 2209, are bound by the penalty, unless otherwise expressly stated. Hence the following come under the penalty of the law; those who agree to cooperate in the same offense by united physical action; accomplices in a crime that of its nature demands complicity; the *mandans,* i. e., the principal author of the crime, and all who furthered its consummation, or concurred in it, if without their aid the crime would not have been committed.

Many persons, however, cannot very well concur physically in the one crime of joining the Masons; the joining is done by the individual joining, and therefore, the first part of Canon 2209 has no place in this discussion.

An accomplice is not necessarily postulated in joining a society; it is true that those who initiate the candidate, or induct him into the society, might be said to be his accomplices. These persons, nevertheless, do not *de facto* commit the same offense the joiner commits. They receive him, he joins. It is the joining that is censured, and is the canonical

---

[16] Prummer, *Manuale Theo. Mor.,* III, p. 355, No. 516.

[17] *Censurae Vigentes,* p. 107, No. 55.

[18] Cf. Vermeersch-Creusen, *Epitome Iur. Can.,* III, p. 277; Ayrinhac, *Penal Legislation,* p. 241, No. 257; Genicot-Salsmans, *Inst. Theo. Mor.,* II, p. 561.

crime.[19]   In crimes of complicity, both accomplices commit
the same crime; in adultery, both sin against chastity and
justice; in a duel, both are duelling; both defile, in sacrilegous
matrimony, a sacred thing.   Not so in joining, and receiving
a member.   Hence paragraph two of Canon 2209 does not
apply here.

Those spoken of in the third paragraph of Canon 2209
might easily concur in the violation of Canon 2335. There
could be a *mandans*, viz., one commanding others to join
the Masons in abuse of some authority, domestic or other.
One also might induce another to join, promising money,
or other temporal advantage, or threatening him with some
loss, or danger.   Again, some one could communicate with
the society, thus enabling the candidate to join.   All these
cases, except that of the *mandans,* are based on the assump-
tion that the society would not, or could not, have been joined
without their cooperation.   Granted that some persons co-
operated in these ways, and that the new member would not
have become a member without their coöperation, then Canon
2231 would bind them under the censure of Canon 2335.

There is an important question that would naturally arise
here.   Do those who join the society in good faith incur the
censure?   The principles of moral theology and ethics concerning ignorance must be applied in the case, and the Code
actually does apply them to all penalties in canon 2229.
Affected ignorance of either the law or the penalty excuses
from no *ipso facto* penalty; crass, or supine ignorance, does
not exempt one from any *latae sententiae* penalty; in-
vincible ignorance excuses from medicinal, but not vindica-
tive *latae sententiae* penalties.   Hence one joining the
Masons in good faith, invincibly ignorant of their condemnation and censure, would not incur excommunication, for
the censure of Canon 2335 is medicinal.

[19] Chelodi, *Ius Poenale*, p. 90, No. 71; "delictum canonicum est eis
nomen dare".

Suppose a person joined in good faith, either as a non-Catholic, or as a Catholic invincibly ignorant of the condemnation and censure, and later, learning of the excommunication and censure, refused to withdraw; would he incur excommunication?

Unfortunately a great many eminent writers establish a censure in this instance. D'Annibale says that such a member escapes censure if he remains unwillingly, that he incurs it if he stays in the society willingly, but he gives no reason for his opinion.[20] Lehmkuhl thinks that the censure would not be incurred immediately on refusing to quit the society after learning of the condemnation and censure, but that it would be incurred when the member first placed an act proving him a member of the sect.[21] Noldin, both in the pre-Code edition of his work " De Poenis Ecclesiasticis ",[22] and in the post-Code edition by Schöneger,[23] is of the same opinion as d'Annibale. Cappello has it that the member certainly would contract excommunication, if he had no reason excusing him from withdrawing, and that he would not incur the censure, if he remained in the society to escape grave harm.[24] Farrugia agrees with Cappello, and, like him, quotes Lehmkuhl as his authority.[25] Cerato holds likewise, but appeals to the instruction of the Holy Office to the Bishops of the world of May 10, 1884, which does not seem to refer to the point under discussion.[26] Cocchi says that if one joined in good faith, and later, learning the truth, externally com-

---

[20] *Summula Theo. Mor.*, I, p. 386, No. 391, nota 4.

[21] *Theologia Moralis,* ed. 12a, II, p. 703, No. 1125.

[22] Ed. 7a, p. 67, No. 75.

[23] Ed. 13a, p. 68, No. 75.

[24] *De Censuris,* p. 268, No. 296.

[25] *Commentarium in Censuras C. I. C.,* pp. 70-71.

[26] *Censurae Vigentes,* p. 107, No. 55; *C. I. C. Fontes,* IV, p. 415, No. 1085.

municated with his associates " ad rimandum id quod bona fide fecerat ", he also would incur the censure.[27]

However, Chelodi rightly avers that the canonical offense is *to join* the societies.[28] Hence one who remained in such societies after having joined in good faith, would not incur the censure.

Regula XV of the *Regulae Iuris* prescribes " odiosa restringi, favores autem ampliari oportet ", and XLIX, " in poenis benignior est interpretatio facienda ". The latter has been incorporated into the Code as the first part of Canon 2219, and is further elaborated in the third part of that canon :—" Non licet poenam de persona ad personam, vel de casu ad casum producere, quamvis par adsit ratio, imo gravior ".

By a censure is punished only an external offense, grave and consummated, conjoined with contumacy. When a law is violated in good faith, contumacy is lacking, and the law is not formally but only materially violated. When a man joins the Masons in good faith, he does not incur the excommunication. Canon 2335 places under censure only *nomen dantes.* Can one who has already joined be called a " nomen dans "? The dictionary equivalent of *nomen dare* is *to be enrolled, to enlist, to join.*[29] The equivalent, then, of *nomen dans* would be one enlisting, enrolling, or joining. Having once enlisted, or joined, he would be no longer a *nomen dans,* but one *qui nomen dedit.* That this interpretation is correct is shown even by those who hold the opposite opinion: d'Annibale says to an objection that he does not answer that *nomen dantes* is

---

[27] Cocchi, *Com. in Cod. Iur. Can.,* VIII, p. 267, No. 171.

[28] Chelodi, *Ius Poenale,* p. 90, No. 71 : " delictum canonicum est eis nomen dare ".

[29] Cf. Leverett's *Latin Lexicon,* s. v. " nomen ".

in the present tense.[30]   To have already joined is in the past tense.   And others, like Farrugia, Lehmkuhl, Noldin, and Ayrinhac, imply confirmingly that the one who has already joined is no longer a *nomen dans,* when they try to convict him of censure on placing what they call a new act as **a** member of the censured society, or on refusing to withdraw, when his good faith is lost.   If he were still a *nomen dans,* they would not have to appeal to this new act, or refusal to withdraw in order to have the censure affect him.

Since, then, *nomen dans* cannot be applied to one who has already joined a sect condemned under censure, and since it is forbidden to extend a penalty from one case to another, it remains that one who joins the societies in good faith, and later on, having that good faith destroyed, does not withdraw, would not come under the excommunication of canon 2335, even though he violates the law against condemned societies just as much, perhaps, as one who joins in bad faith.[31]

Secta is from *sequor* and is given as a manner of action, rule, method of life; it was used by Cicero as meaning a party, or faction, for example, " secta philosophorum ".[32] Up to the fourth century after Christ, it had both a good and bad significance,[33] but, after that time, the latter meaning seems to have prevailed,[34] and is still used thus.   In conjunction with *massonica* it is here used to signify " illa " Massonica secta quae ab Apostolica Sede a tempore Clementis XII usque ad tempora nostra pluries damnata fuit ".[35]   It

---

[30] *Sum. Theo. Mor.,* I, p. 386, No. 391, nota 4.

[31] Cf. Schaef, *Cloister,* p. 90, for a similar case.

[32] Cf. Leverett, s. v. " secta ".

[33] Cf. Calvinus, *Lexicon Magnum,* s. v. " secta ".

[34] Christopher, S. Aurelii Augustini. . . . *De Catechizandis Rudibus,* Liber Unus, Translation and Commentary, p. 330.

[35] Cocchi, *Com. in Cod. Iur. Can.,* VIII, p. 267, No. 170.

is that international organization, or system of societies known as the Freemasons, Franc-Maçons, i Liberi Murati, Freimaurer, Masoni, etc.

Aliisve eiusdem generis associationibus is interpreted by Genicot as meaning:—"quaecumque sectae eiusdem generis, vid. quaecumque vel contra Ecclesiam, vel contra legitimas civiles potestates machinantur". He goes on to say that *secta* supposes the associates are united by a closed union, i. e., *arcto foedere*; that it is *aliquo modo* secret, either regarding the leaders and the members, or regarding the means and teachings of the society, even though the purpose may be known to all, and no oath of secrecy is exacted.[36]

Simon asserts that it means "similar (*secret*) societies that plot against the Church or against legitimate civil authority.[37] But the Pre-Code[38] edition of Noldin's *De Poenis Ecclesiasticis* and the Post-Code by Schöneger state that for a society to be prohibited under censure it is required that it be similar to Freemasonry both as to its end, and also as to its secret organization, that the sect have secret statutes and that it be ruled by occult leaders.[39]

Vermeersch-Creusen hold that a society must have the two notes of secrecy and conspiracy against civil, or ecclesiastical authority to come under this canon.[40] Although Lehmkuhl at one time held that anti-social societies, whether secret or not, came under the censure against the Masons and societies *eiusdem generis*,[41] he changed his mind

[36] Genicot-Salsmans, *Inst. Theo. Mor.*, II, p. 560, No. 594.

[37] Faculties of Pastors and Confessors for Absolution and Dispensation, p. 40, No. 2.

[38] *De Poenis Ecclesiasticis*, ed. 7a, p. 66, No. 74.

[39] *De Poenis Ecclesiasticis*, ed. 13a, p. 66, No. 74.

[40] *Epitome Iur. Can.*, III, p. 276, No. 535.

[41] *Theo. Mor.* ed. 12a, II, p. 702, No. 1224.

later, and said that to be of the same genus as the Masons a sect had to be like that society in organization, direction and purpose, and be ruled by occult leaders.[42]

The question therefore arises, is secrecy an essential note of Freemasonry, and must an anti-social society have it to be *eiusdem generis* as the Masonic sect?

Vermeersch, while giving no reason for his opinion in his Epitome, does however give his reasons at length in his work " De Prohibitione et Censura Librorum ". That secrecy is the *genus* of the societies in question, he says, is shown both by the constant usage of Pontifical documents and the common acceptation of authorities.[43]

It is certainly true that the Masons are a secret society, yet so are the Odd Fellows, the Knights of Pythias, and the Sons of Temperance. The first is condemned under censure, the other societies are not. If the note of secrecy rendered a society of the same nature as the Masons, why are the Knights of Pythias and the other two societies not condemned in the same manner as the Masons, since they would be *eiusdem generis*? Is not, therefore, secrecy an accidental, rather than an essential note of Freemasonry, and the real *genus* of that craft the conspiracy for which it is censured?

Concerning Vermeersch's argument that the constant usage of Pontifical documents demonstrates that secrecy is an essential note of Freemasonry, it cannot be found anywhere that the Holy See expressly states that it is. In the several constitutions against Freemasonry and the Carbonari, the Popes, speaking about these sects, do call them secret sects, *sectae occultae,* which as a matter of fact they were, or are. But while this secrecy might be one of the reasons of their condemnation, the reason they were placed under

[42] *Casus Conscientiae,* ed. 1913, pp. 556-558.

[43] *De Prohibitione et Censura Librorum,* ed. 2a, p. 62, seq., ix.

censure, as was later declared,[44] was their conspiracy against Church or State.

Furthermore, the Sacred Congregation of the Holy Office, contrary to what Vermeersch believes, did not define that the sects condemned by Pontifical Constitutions were, in the first place, occult societies, *societates occultas.* The question proposed was this:—" Quaenam sint societates damnatae in pontificiis constitutionibus "? The answer,—" Societates occultae, de quibus in pontificiis constitutionibus sermo est, eae omnes intelliguntur quae adversus Ecclesiam vel gubernium sibi aliquid proponunt, exigant vel non exigant a suis assechs iuramentum de secreto servando ".[45] The question asked, Which societies are condemned? was not answered. What was said was that the occult societies spoken of in the pontifical constitutions were to be understood as all those which proposed to themselves anything against either Church or State. Indeed this very response argues against the contrary opinion, for, far from saying that the societies condemned by the pontifical constitutions were, in the first place, secret societies, it expressly stated that it made no difference whether the societies exacted from their members or not, an oath of secrecy. It is by this very oath that secret societies insure their secrecy.

Again Vermeersch objects that although the Holy Office, in the instruction of May 10, 1884, declares that the oath of secrecy is not required, nevertheless in the same article it treated of denouncing the occult leaders, which, he claims, hints of secrecy. In reality this instruction does not treat in that same article, or in any of its articles, of denouncing the occult leaders of the sects.[46] And even if it did treat of

[44] Cf. *Inst. S. C. S. Off.*, 10 Maii, 1884, paragraph 3, *C. I. C. Fontes*, IV, p. 415, No. 1085.

[45] *S. C. S. Off.*, 5 Aug. 1846; *C. I. C. Fontes*, IV, p. 177, No. 899.

[46] The article referred to is as follows:—" Ne quis vero errori locus

the denunciation of occult leaders, as it does not, might it not easily mean that these occult leaders had to be denounced, if there were any such in the society? Taking, moreover this phrase, *earumve occultos coriphaeos ac duces non denunciantes,* as found in the constitution " Apostolicae Sedis ", could not a society be non-secret and yet have some hidden leader, or director? [47] It is, after all, the secrecy that can be revealed to no one, not even to those who have a right to know it, that makes a society a secret society,[48] and the circumstance that the leaders of a society were unknown would hardly make it a secret society in the above sense.

Vermeersch says that the phrase of the constitution " Apostolicae Sedis ", *seu palam seu clandestine* does not weaken his opinion, " nam ex ipso Leone XIII, in encycl. ' Humanum Genus ', ' Ecclesiae sanctae perniciem palam aperteque moliuntur ' (Francomurarii), et infra subiungitur ' re penitus perspecta genus societatum clandestinarum moremque retinent ' ". It was and is the case that Freemasonry openly and manifestly machinates against God's Holy Church. But who will deny that they also secretly and hiddenly conspire against it? And whilst *palam seu clandestine* may refer only to *the manner of acting,* still the charge against them is that they *act against the Church.* Granting that the *palam seu clandestine* may refer only

fiat, cum diiudicandum erit, quaenam ex his perniciosis sectis censurae, quae vero prohibitioni tantum obnoxiae sint, certum imprimis est, excommunicatione latae sententiae massonicam aliisque eiusdem generis sectis quae capite 2, n. 4. Pontificiae Constitutionis 'Apostolicae Sedis' designantur, quaeque contra Ecclesiam vel legitimas potestates machinantur, sive id clam sive palam fecerint, sive exigerint sive non a suis asseclis, secreti servandi iuramentum ". Cf. *C. I. C. Fontes,* IV, p. 415, No. 1085.

[47] Cf. *C. I. C. Fontes,* III, p. 27, No. 552.

[48] Cf. S. C. S. Off., 10 Maii, 1884; *C. I. C. Fontes,* IV, p. 417, No. 1085, paragraph 4, " secretum nemini pandendum ".

to the manner of acting, yet the phrase of the instruction of the Holy Office, " exigant vel non exigant a suis asseclis iuramentum de secreto servando ", as has already been pointed out, shows that secrecy is not an essential note,[49] for the oath of secrecy is synonymous with secrecy.

And now what societies are meant by the other phrase quoted by Father Vermeersch, " re penitus perspecta, genus societatum clandestinarum moremque retinent? " The reference and its context is the following:

There are several organized bodies which, though differing in name, in ceremonial, in form and origin, are nevertheless so bound together by community of purpose and by the similarity of their main opinions, as to make in fact one thing with the sect of the Freemasons, which is a kind of centre whence they all go forth, and whither they all return. Now, these no longer show a desire to remain concealed; for they hold their meetings in the daylight and before the public eye, and publish their own newspaper organs; and yet, when thoroughly understood, they are found still to retain the nature and habits of secret societies.[50]

The translator of the above rendered, *societatum clandestinarum—of secret societies;* a much better translation would have been the literal one, *clandestine societies.* It must be remembered that there is great confusion of terms in the treatment of condemned societies, and as Könings well remarks, these anti-social societies are improperly termed occult, or secret societies.[51] It cannot be the secrecy enshrouding these societies that makes them one with Freemasonry, for further down in the same article Pope Leo says that candidates are *generally* commanded to promise, or swear, absolute secrecy. They are, therefore,

---

[49] 10 Maii, 1884; *C. I. C. Fontes,* IV, p. 417, No. 1085.
[50] From *The Great Encyclicals of Leo XIII,* " Freemasonry " p. 87.
[51] Könings, *Theo. Mor.,* II, p. 346, No. 1721.

not always made to do so. Hence it must be that the fact which makes them similar to the sect of Freemasons is the community of purpose and the similarity of their main opinions. These societies are also said to differ in origin, name, form and ceremonial; might not the secret organization be considered the form of one and not of another? And whilst their leaders can be hidden, it does not necessarily follow that they are.

That the open or clandestine machination may, perhaps refer only to the scope of the societies in question, is also asserted by Vermeersch, and he says the Holy Office had to answer (debuit respondere) in its response of August 21, 1850 that it made no difference that the society profess it did not conspire against Church or state. Really the response did not say that. The instance has already been treated. Bishop Kenrick asked whether those societies which, although they entered into a secret union binding themselves by oath, nevertheless declared that they did not conspire against Church or State, were to be considered strictly forbidden, and again whether those secret societies whose members are bound by oath, or other solemn promise, are to be considered forbidden, by reason that they admit their organizations are secret, yet deny that their object is contrary to the state, or to religion.[52] The answer was that these societies were comprehended in the Pontifical Constitutions,—" Comprehendi in Pontificiis Constitutionibus ".[53]

All the arguments adduced by Father Vermeersch show but one thing, that the Freemasons, a sect that machinates against the Church and State, and is censured for so doing, is *de facto* a secret society; they do not prove that secrecy is a note necessary for incurring the excommunication; and

[52] Cf. *Conc. Plen. Balt. II, Acta et Decreta,* appendix xxviii.

[53] *Conc. Plen. Balt. II, Acta et Decreta,* appendix xxviii, Cf. Pennachi, *Com. in Const. Apos. Sed.,* I, p. 615.

hence they do not prove that *eiusdem generis* is not explained by the clause that follows, in both the constitution "Apostolicae Sedis,"[54] and in canon 2335, *quae contra Ecclesiam vel legitimas civiles potestates machinantur.*[55]

Nor is the opinion fostered by Vermeersch as common as he would have us believe. Of those who wrote before the Code, Nilles,[56] d'Annibale,[57] Sabetti,[58] Bucceroni,[59] Lehmkuhl (in his earlier editions),[60] Ballerini,[61] Genicot (also in his earlier editions)[62] Bargilliat,[63] and Aertnys,[64] did not hold his view. And of the Post-Code authors, Blat,[65] Ayrinhac,[66] Farrugia,[67] Sole,[68] Pighi,[69] Eichman,[70] Pistocchi,[71] Prummer,[72] Tanquerey,[73] Cappello,[74] and Cippolini[75]

[54] Cf. *C. I. C. Fontes,* III, p. 27, No. 552.

[55] The exact wording of the constitution "Apostolicae Sedis" is "quae contra Ecclesiam vel legitimas potestates seu palam seu clandestine machinantur."

[56] *Commentaria in Con. Plen. Balt. III,* II, pp. 308-309.

[57] *Sum. Theo. Mor.,* I, p. 358, nota 4.

[58] *Compendium Theo. Mor.,* ed. 12a, p. 780, No. 993.

[59] *Inst. Theo. Mor.,* ed. 6a, IV, p. 234, No. 1186.

[60] *Theologia Moralis,* ed. 5a, II, p. 697, No. 950.

[61] *Opus Theo. Mor.,* ed. 3a, III, p. 274, No. 302.

[62] *Inst. Theo. Mor.,* (1897), II, p. 762, No. 596.

[63] *Praelectiones Iur. Can.,* ed. 14a, II, p. 530.

[64] *Theo. Mor.,* ed. 3a, II, p. 399, No. 93.

[65] *Com. Cod. Iur. Can.,* V, p. 225, No. 176.

[66] *Penal Legislation,* p. 241, No. 257.

[67] *Com. in Tex. Cod. Iur. Can.,* p. 68, No. 83.

[68] *De Delictis et Poenis,* p. 269.

[69] *Censurae Latae Sententiae,* ed. 5a, p. 31, No. 74.

[70] *Das Strafrecht des Codex Iuris Canonici,* (1920) pp. 150-151.

[71] *I Canoni Penali,* p. 102.

[72] *Man. Theo. Mor.,* III, p. 355.

[73] *Synopsis Theo. Mor.,* II, p. 689, No. 1184.

[74] *De Censuris,* ed. 2a, pp. 268-269.

[75] *De Censuris Latae Sententiae,* p. 134.

differ from him. Surely these are enough to show that Vermeersch's opinion is not the commonly accepted one.

Some others claim [76] as a necessary note of the societies censured by canon 2355 that the members be united in a closed union, *ut arcto foedere socii uniantur*. Those who uphold this appeal to the constitution " In Eminenti " of Clement XII, and to the encyclical " Humanum Genus " of Leo XIII. The Pontiffs in these constitutions are speaking of Freemasonry, and it is again the case that a feature of one society is pointed out by the Holy See, but by no means declared a necessary note for that society, or other societies, to come under the censure against societies that conspire against the ecclesiastical or civil authority.[77]

Augustine finds a shade of difference in the meaning of the term *sectis* as used in the constitution " Apostolicae Sedis ",[78] and *associationibus* as used in canon 2335. He says :—

Note the word " association ", which is different from " sect ", the term employed in the " Apostolicae Sedis ". Association admits of a wider range. It does not necessarliy mean a " closed " or compact society, with statutes or by-laws, but merely a union of individuals for a definite purpose.[79]

An association is defined by lexicographers as " a union of persons in a company or society for some particular purpose ".[80] A sect in reality does not mean a closed or compact society, with statutes or by-laws. It means those following

[76] E. g. Genicot-Salsmans, II, p. 560, No. 594; Vermeersch, *De Prohibitione et Censura Librorum,* ed. 2a, p. 62, seq.

[77] Cf. *C. I. C. Fontes,* I, p. 656, No. 299, paragraph 1; III, p. 224. No. 591, paragraph 7.

[78] Cf. C. II, n. 4. "Apostolicae Sedis", *C. I. C. Fontes,* III. p. 27, No. 552.

[79] *Commentary,* VIII, pp. 341-342.

[80] Cf. Webster's *Unabridged Dictionary,* s. v. " association ".

a particular leader, or authority, or attached to a certain opinion; a company or set having a common belief, or allegiance distinct from others; in religion, the believers in a particular creed, or the upholders of a particular practice, and especially, in modern times, a party dissenting from an established church of a denomination; in philosophy, the disciples of a particular master; a school; in society and the state, an order, rank, class, or party.[81]

There is no such word as " associatio " in classical Latin; it is first met in an edict of Philip IV, of the year 1301.[82] It is evidently a modern term, and its significance is not to be found in the older use of the word " associare ", but in the modern use of the word itself. As has been seen, in English an association is a union of persons in a company or society for some particular purpose.[83] In the sense of society, an association may be defined as a number of persons associated for any temporal or permanent object.[84] Hence, if either of the words sect, or association, is stronger than the other, it is association, and not sect. Indeed throughout the legislation concerning condemned societies the Holy See uses indiscriminately the terms *societas* and *secta*.[85] *Societas* and *associatio* are identical in meaning, and the Code uses *secta* in Canon 683 : 1, *societas* in 1065 : 1, and *associatio* in 684, all in the sense of a union of persons for some common purpose. It remains, then, that a closed, or compact union is not necessarily postulated by the word *secta*. In passing, however, let it be said that an association or society without some sort of constitution, or by-laws is hard to conceive.

---

[81] Cf. Webster's *Unabridged Dictionary,* s. v. " sect ".

[82] Du Cange, *Glossarium Mediae et Infimae Latinitatis,* a. s. " associatio ".

[83] Webster's *Unabridged Dictionary,* s. v. " association ".

[84] Cf. Webster's *Unabridged Dictionary,* s. v. " society ".

[85] Cf. Canons 693 : 1; 1065 : 1; 1240 : 1 : 1; 1399 : 8; & 1453 : 1.

Cappello interprets the clause, *quae contra Ecclesiam,* etc., as meaning against the teaching, authority, constitutive form of the Church, and even ecclesiastical persons as such.[86] Sole does likewise,[87] and Cippolini adds to their enumeration, *contra iura et praerogativa.*[88] Cerato, on the other hand, thinks that the canon does not intend *contra eius doctrinam et personas ecclesiasticas qua tales,* although he admits *contra societatem Ecclesiae, eiusque legitimas potestatem et societatis et potestatis constitutionem.*[89] It is well to remember that the Holy See has given us some inkling of what is meant by the phrase " quae contra Ecclesiam what is meant by the phrase *quae contra Ecclesiam machinantur.* It is evident from the constitution " Ecclesiam " of Pius VII,[90] from " Quo Graviora " from the allocution " Multiplices Inter "[91] and the encyclical " Quamquam Dolores " of Pius IX,[92] that an attempt to overthrow the doctrines of the Church is considered by the Pontiffs mentioned as a real machination against the Church. D'Annibale points out that the Holy Office declared, August 5, 1846, that the societies condemned under censure were " eae omnes . . . quae adversus Ecclesiam vel gubernium sibi *aliquid* proponunt ", and he interprets this as meaning anything against the doctrines, discipline and rights of the Church.[93]

" *Vel legitimas civiles potestates* " includes all societies that conspire or plot against the State or government, i. e., against

[86] *De Censuris,* ed. 2a, p. 270, No. 299.

[87] *De Delictis et Poenis,* p. 269; cf. d'Annibale, *Sum. Theo. Mor.,* I, p. 385, nota 4.

[88] *De Censuris Latae Sententiae,* p. 136, No. 140.

[89] *Censurae Vigentes.* p. 109, No. 105.

[90] 13 Sept. 1821; *C. I. C. Fontes,* II, pp. 722-723, No. 479, paragraph 5.

[91] 25 Sept., 1865, *C. I. C. Fontes,* II, p. 1009, No. 544.

[92] 29 Maii, 1873, *C. I. C. Fontes,* III, p. 70, No. 563.

[93] *Sum. Theo. Mor.,* I, p. 385, nota 4.

lawful civil authority,[94] as d'Annibale says, "quae aliquid moliuntur . . . quod a forma legitimi regiminis aut a iure civitatis publico alienum sit ".[95]

" Machinantur " signifies to conspire, or plot: " scilicet . . . qui data opera seu ex fine (vel ex instituto vel saltem de facto [96]) quem prosequuntur contra Ecclesiam vel rempublicam conspirant, sive palam sive clandestine, sive verbis vel scriptis, hac aliave ratione ".[97]

Which societies are, therefore, to be considered as conspiring against the Church, or State? Cappello gives the following catalogue:—" praeter massonicam ", 1. societas ' carbonaria '; 2. societas ' fenianorum '; societas ' nihilistica ' et ' anarchistica ' ut patet ex fine quem prosequuntur ".[98] The Carbonari and Fenians need be mentioned no longer, for they have been out of existence for many years.[99] Anarchistic and nihilistic societies, certainly, would fall under censure, because of their purpose, the overthrowing of all existing forms of government, and of all government entirely.

Despite what many writers hold about the Odd Fellows, the Knights of Pythias, the Sons of Temperance, and the Independent Order of Good Templars, those who join these societies do not incur the excommunication of canon 2335, although they are guilty of grave sin. Augustine, it is feared, confounds the Independent Order of Good Templars with the Knights Templars. The latter are really Masons,[100] the

[94] Cf. Pius VII in " Ecclesiam ", 13 Sep., 1921, *C. I. C. Fontes*, II, p. 723.

[95] *Sum. Theo. Mor.*, I, p. 385, No. 391, nota 4.

[96] Chelodi, *Ius Poenale,* p. 90, No. 71.

[97] Cappello, *De Censuris,* p. 271, No. 300.

[98] *De Censuris,* p. 269, No. 298.

[99] Corbett's " Carbonari ", *Cath. Ency.*, III, p. 331; Preuss, *Dict. of Secret and Other Societies,* p. 125.

[100] Preuss, *Dict. of Secret and Other Societies,* p. 241.

former are not masonic, and have never been placed under censure.[101]

It does not seem to be true that Negro Masons escape censure. They are, after all, Masons, Masonic descendants of Prince Hall, who was made a Mason by an English Lodge in Boston, in 1775. The fact that White Masons declare their colored brethren are " spurious ", or " irregular ", and refuse to recognize them does not make the Negro Masons any the less Masons; no one would dare say that the members of the Grand Orient of France are not Masons because they have been repudiated and excommunicated by English, American and German Grand Lodges.[102]

It can hardly be doubted that the Order of de Molay is affiliated to Masonry. Whilst it is true the Order of de Molay cannot be called a Masonic organization in the strictest sense of the word, still it was founded by Freemasons, for the sons of Freemasons; any Master Mason may visit the chapters of the order and witness the " work "; and any recognized Masonic body of either York or Scottish jurisdiction may sponsor a de Molay chapter.[103] Just as those who enter a cremation society affiliated to Freemasonry incur the same penalty as the Freemasons [104] and, on the declaration of the Apostolic Delegation, female societies affiliated to societies already nominally condemned by the Church fall under the same condemnations as the male societies,[105] so it would seem that youths who join the Order of de Molay are

---

[101] Cf. Augustine, *Commentary*, VIII, pp. 343-344; Preuss, *American Freemasonry*, p. 421; *S. C. S. Off.*, Aug. 9, 1893, *C. I. C. Fontes*, IV, p. 482, No. 1167.

[102] Gruber, " Masonry ", *Cath. Ency.*, IX, p. 774.

[103] Preuss, *Dict. of Secret and Other Societies*, pp. 349-350.

[104] Cf. *S. C. S. Off.*, 19 Maii, 1886; *C. I. C. Fontes,* IV, p. 428, No. 1100.

[105] Apostolic Delegation, Washington, Aug. 2, 1907, answer No. 15, 352-C.

subject to the censure of canon 2335.[106]   However, the Church has not nominally condemned the de Molay as yet, and, therefore, according to the Third Plenary Council of Baltimore, the above opinion, that those who join incur excommunication, cannot be stated as certain.   Whether or not those who join the Order of de Molay incur excommunication depends on whether the society is affiliated to Freemasonry, or not.[107]

Many of the older writers considered the members of Bible Societies as coming under this censure as it obtained in the constitution " Apostolicae Sedis ".   Even at the present time, some consider it an unsettled question,[108] and some believe that those who join these societies are *ipso facto* excommunicated by canon 2335.[109]   Noldin, however, rightly says that Bible Societies, while condemned, are not *sub censura*.[110]

In none of the Papal letters or constitutions against them can it be found that they were actually condemned under censure, although they were repeatedly condemned.[111]   If Gregory XVI in his constitution " Inter Praecipuas " does

---

[106] The society is open only to boys over 16 years of age; hence they can incur censure.   Canon 2230.

[107] Cf. *Conc. Plen. Balt. III, Acta et Decreta,* tit. VIII, c. iii, n. 1, No. 255.

[108] Cf. Cappello, *De Censuris,* p. 269, No. 298.

[109] Cf. Farrugia, *Com. in Censuras Latae Sententiae,* p. 68, No. 83; " Sub huius societatis nomine veniunt . . . societates biblicae ".

[110] Noldin-Schöneger, *De Poenis Ecclesiasticis,* p. 66, No. 74.

[111] Cf. " Postremis Litteris ", Pii VII, de Martinis *Iuris Pontificii* (Partes), IV, p. 14; " Magno et Acerbo ", Pii VII, Denz.-Bann, *Enchiridion,* p. 423, No. 1602-1606; Epistola S. C. P. F., *C. I. C. Fontes,* II, p. 800, No. 502, nota 6; " Ubi Primum " Leonis XII, 21 Maii, 1824, *Bull. Rom. Con.,* XIII. p. 57; " Traditi ", Pii VIII, 21, Maii, 1829, *Bull. Rom. Con.* XIV, p. 23; " Inter Praecipuas " Gregorii XVI, 5, Maii, 1844, *C. I. C. Fontes,* II, p. 797, No. 502, 11-13, " Qui Pluribus " Pii IX, 9 Novembris, 1846, *C. I. C. Fontes,* II, p. 802, No. 504.

declare that " inter machinationes, quibus nostra hac aetate acatholici diversorum nominum insidiari cultoribus catholicae veritatis, earumque animos a sanctitate fidei avertere conituntur, haud ultimum tenet locum societates biblicae ",[112] it is clear from the context that the machination meant is not that *contra Ecclesiam vel civiles potestates*[113] " quae ad legitimos principatus labefactandos et Ecclesiam funditus delendam spectant ",[114] carried on by the Masons and similar sects. The Pontiff means that machination that perverts Catholic hearts, and proselytizes the poor and ignorant. Hence those who join Bible societies do not incur the excommunication of this canon. Whatever penalties the Church has decreed in canon 2318 against "auctores et editores qui sine debita licentia sacrarum Scripturarum libros vel earum adnotationes aut commentarios imprimi curant ", are of no interest here, since they are incurred by these persons as individuals, and not as members of condemned societies.

The Young Men's Christian Association, popularly known as the " Y ", does not seem to be condemned, to say nothing of condemned under censure.[115]

There are other societies concerning which writers cannot agree whether they are condemned under censure or not. Let it be said with Bargilliat that aside from the declarations of the Holy See, and, for the United States, of the Commission on Condemned Societies, whether or not a society is condemned under censure can be told by those who are members, " nempe si his exploratum sit societatem cui

---

[112] *C. I. C. Fontes,* II, p. 797, No. 502, paragraph 1.

[113] Cf. Canon 2335; const. " Apostolicae Sedis ", C. II, n. 4, *C. I. C. Fontes,* III, p. 27, No. 552.

[114] *C. I. C. Fontes,* II, p. 727, No. 481, paragraph 11.

[115] Cf. *Acta Apostolicae Sedis,* XII, p. 595; also *Time,* IX, n. 15, p. 21 (April 11, 1927).

nomen dederunt aliquid contra Ecclesiam vel civile Gubernium, machinari ".[116]

Those who join, therefore, the Masons, or societies of the
same kind contract *ipso facto* excommunication.   Excommunication is a censure by which one is excluded from
communion with the faithful with the concomitant canonical
effects.[117]   The effects of excommunication are exclusion
from divine services,[118] from the sacraments and sacramentals,[119] from the administration of the sacraments and sacramentals,[120] from enjoying the indulgences, suffrages, public
prayers, and for *vitandi* of having Holy Mass applied to
them, except for their conversion;[121] removal from legal
ecclesiastical acts, and the suspension of certain other rights;
an excommunicate cannot act in ecclesiastical causes, is prohibited to exercise ecclesiastical offices and functions, and to
enjoy privileges previously granted by the Church.[122]   Under
the name of legal acts comes the exercise of all those offices
mentioned in canon 2256:2.   They are the administration
of ecclesiastical property, and the exercise of the offices of
judge, auditor, relator, defensor of the bond, promotor of
justice and faith, notary, chancellor, cursor, apparitor, advocate, or procurator, in ecclesiastical causes, of sponsors at
Baptism and Confirmation,[123] of the right to vote in ecclesiastical elections, and of the right of patronage.   All acts of
jurisdiction in the external forum are illicit, if posited by one
excommunicated *ipso facto;* invalid, if performed by one

[116] Bargilliat, *Prae. Iur. Can.*, II, p. 313, No. 1375 (b).

[117] Canon 2257: 1.

[118] Canon 2259.

[119] Canon 2260.

[120] Canon 2261.

[121] Canon 2262.

[122] Canon 2263.

[123] Cf. Kearney, *Sponsors at Baptism*, p. 86.

excommunicated by a damnatory, or declaratory sentence, except in the danger of death.[124] Excommunicated persons cannot lawfully exercise the right of electing, presenting, or nominating; if they are excommunicated by a damnatory or declaratory sentence they cannot do so validly; they cannot receive dignities, offices, benefices, ecclesiastical pensions, or other functions in the Church, nor can they be promoted to Orders.[125] After a damnatory or declaratory sentence, they are deprived of the income of all dignities, offices, benefices, pensions, and *vitandi* are deprived of the dignity, office, benefice, pension, or function itself.[126] *Vitandi* are also excluded from social intercourse with the faithful; not however with their wives, parents, children, servants, subjects, or those whom a reasonable cause excuses.[127]

The censure of canon 2335 is reserved *simpliciter* to the Holy See. Censures are reserved to the Holy See *simpliciter, speciali modo* and *specialissimo modo,* just as the bond of reservation is more easily, or more strictly observed.[128] Censures reserved *simpliciter* are, therefore, reserved in the first degree of reservation. By the Holy See, or the Apostolic See is meant not only the Holy Father himself, but according to the nature, or context of the law, the various congregations, tribunals, and offices through which the Pontiff expedites the affairs of the Church. As shall be seen below, this excommunication is reserved to the Congregation of the Holy Office, for the external forum, and the Sacred Penitentiary, also, for the internal forum.

The question of the Orientals is somewhat perplexing. Canon One exempts the Orientals from the law of the Code,

[124] Canon 2264.
[125] Canon 2265.
[126] Canon 2266.
[127] Canon 2267.
[128] Cf. Cappello, *De Censuris,* p. 6, No. 4.

except in those things which of their nature affect them also. Hence, it would seem, at first sight, that the Orientals are not bound by the legislation concerning Freemasonry and other condemned societies.

In 1867 the Section of the Congregation of the Propaganda on Oriental Affairs addressed a letter to the Apostolic Delegates and Bishops of the Oriental countries, in which surprise was expressed that it was even doubted that the Oriental Masons were condemned and under excommunication. So grave were the nature of the matter and the Apostolic condemnations that it seemed impossible that any Christians were exempt, no matter of what nation, place, time or rite. The Congregation pointed out that it had never failed to notify the Oriental Church of the Pontifical decrees against the Masons. To silence all doubts, however, the Holy Office expressly declared that the Orientals were comprehended in the Pontifical constitutions against the Masons, and that they were even affected by the penalties contained in the same constitutions.[129]

In the meantime the constitution " Apostolicae Sedis " had been promulgated, and some difficulty arose concerning its application to the Orientals. In a letter to the Apostolic Delegates of the Oriental countries, dealing itself with the application of the *missa pro populo,* the Propaganda declared that according to the decree of Innocent III in the Fourth Lateran Council, " Licet Graecos ",[130] and also according to the decision of a congregation of theologians held at the instance of Card. Pamphili, at which the great Lambertini, afterwards Benedict XIV, was present, the pontifical constitutions did not apply to the Oriental Church, except in matters of faith and doctrine, where the matter showed that the Orientals were comprehended insomuch as it was not only

[129] *Collectanea S. C. P. F.,* II, p. 6, No. 1320.
[130] Cap. vi, tit. XLII, de Baptismo, III in X.

of ecclesiastical, but also of divine or natural law, and when the Orientals are expressly mentioned.[131] Whilst this opinion had as yet never received express and formal approbation from the Holy See, the letter continued, still it had its tacit approval, for the Holy See had acted upon it, and never condemned it, though it was known that canonists both held and taught it.

The binding power over the Orientals of the constitution "Apostolicae Sedis" was finally definitely settled, August 6, 1885. The Holy Office, on that date, declared "per constitutionem 'Apostolicae Sedis' nihil esse innovatum circa censuras earumque reservationes pro fidelibus rituum orientalium". There was an exception to this general rule, however, which canonized the teaching of canonists referred to immediately above. The Orientals were subject to all the censures of the constitution on matters of dogma, where they were expressly mentioned, and where the matter showed that they were comprehended, since it was not of mere ecclesiastical law, but of the natural or divine. Furthermore the encyclical made specific reference to the matter at hand; the Orientals were nominally included in all constitutions against those who had joined the Masonic, or similar sects, and were subject to the censure and its reservation for so doing. The matter was, therefore, closed.[132]

Do, however, the Orientals come under Canon 2335? Cicognani thinks that the law of "Apostolicae Sedis" still applies to the Orientals, and that they do not enjoy the mitigations of that law introduced by Canon 2335, although he does not say so directly. It does not seem to be altogether true that they do not enjoy the mitigations of the new law. The whole discussion hinges on the declaration of the Holy Office, August 5, 1885. The declaration does not mean that

---

[131] *Collectanea S. C. P. F.*, II, p. 165, No. 1578.
[132] *Collectanea S. C. P. F.*, II, p. 208, No. 1640.

the constitutions against the Masons and other anti-social societies, promulgated prior to August 5, 1885, are alone to be the legislation for the Orientals thereafter, but it means that whenever there appears any new legislation about Freemasonry for the Latin Church, *natura rei* this is to apply also to the Oriental Church, even, against Cicognani, as their proper legislation, " tanquam propria legislatione ".[133]   The practice of the Holy See has never been known to be stricter with the Orientals than with the Latins; its attitude towards the Eastern Church has always been characterized by consideration and respect.   Hence it is almost absurd to say that Orientals who join, favor, or do not denounce the hidden or occult leaders of, anti-social societies incur a censure that affects only those who join, if they are Latins.   Blat [134] and Augustine are of this opinion.[135]

ARTICLE II. CLERICS AND RELIGIOUS ARE ALSO SUBJECT TO CERTAIN " FERENDAE SENTENTIAE " PUNISHMENTS, AND ARE TO BE DENOUNCED TO THE HOLY OFFICE.   CANON 2336.

1.   CLERICI QUI DELICTUM COMMISERUNT DE QUO IN CAN. 2334, 2335, PRAETER POENAS CITATIS CANONIBUS STATUTAS, POENA SUSPENSIONIS VEL PRIVATIONIS IPSIUS BENEFICII, OFFICII, DIGNITATIS, PENSIONIS VEL MUNERIS, SI QUA FORTE IN ECCLESIA HABEANT: RELIGIOSI AUTEM PRIVATIONEM OFFICII ET VOCIS ACTIVAE ET PASSIVAE ALIISQUE POENIS AD NORMAM CONSTITUTIONUM PLECTANTUR.

2.   INSUPER CLERICI ET RELIGIOSI NOMEN DANTES SECTAE MASSONICAE ALIISQUE SIMILIBUS ASSOCIATIONIBUS DENUNTIARI DEBENT SACRAE CONGREGATIONI S. OFFICII.

[133] Cicognani, p. 11.
[134] Blat., *Com. Cod. Iur. Can.,* V, p. 61.
[135] Augustine, *Commentary,* VIII, p. 343.

The penalties of this canon are all *ferendae sententiae,* and also *indeterminata,* for it is left to the prudence of the judge which is to be applied.[1]

The offence of interest here is that of Canon 2335, and whatever was said in the first article of the present chapter about the conditions under which the canonical offense is committed is also to be kept in mind in the treatment of this canon.

Clerics are those who have received at least the first tonsure.[2] If clerics join anti-social societies, they may be suspended or deprived of the functions mentioned in the canon.

Suspension is a censure by which a cleric is prohibited the exercise of his office or benefice.[3] Privation is the deprival of the office, or benefice.[4] A benefice is a juridical entity consisting of a sacred office and the right of partaking of the income of the endowment attached to the office; it must be erected *in perpetuum* by a competent ecclesiastical authority.[5] An office, in the wide sense, is any function exercised for a spiritual end; in the strict sense, it is a function permanently constituted by divine or ecclesiastical ordination, bringing with it some participation in the ecclesiastical power of order or jurisdiction.[6]

A dignity is a prebendary, to which, besides the prerogative of honor, jurisdiction in the external forum has been attached.[7] The offices of the archpriest, archdeacon,

---

[1] Canon 2217: 1-1 and 2.

[2] Canon 108.

[3] Canon 2278: 1.

[4] Wernz, *Ius Decretalium,* VI, p. 118, No. 115.

[5] Canon 1409.

[6] Canon 145-1.

[7] Vermeersch-Creusen, *Epitome Iur. Can.,* I, p. 260, No. 449.

primicerius, treasurer and chantor are all dignities.[8] A pension is the right of partaking of some of the incomes attached to a benefice, without, however, a perpetual title to it.[9] And a function, or *munus* is an office in the wide sense, i. e., any charge exercised for a spiritual purpose.

Hence, a cleric who joins an anti-social society may be punished by suspension or by privation of any of the offices mentioned.

A religious is one who has taken vows in a religious community,[10] viz., in a society approved by legitimate ecclesiastical authority, in which the members take public vows, and thus tend towards evangelical perfection.[11] Religious who join anti-social societies are to be deprived of office, whether in or outside of the community. They are also to be deprived of active and passive voice, that is the right of voting and of being voted for in canonical elections within the community. And if there are special penalties in the constitutions of the community against joining anti-social societies, they may also be punished by them.

All clerics and religious who join anti-social societies are to be denounced to the Holy Office. This is the last vestige of the obligation of denouncing the members of these societies, the origin and development of which has already been seen in Chapter II, Art. II. Vermeersch-Creusen think that this denunciation is of obligation because of canon 1935 : 2.[12] However, there is no sanction attached to this law, and as the above-mentioned writers themselves say it can easily be presumed that the authorities, e. g., the Ordinary, or religious superior have fulfilled it. How-

---

[8] Cf. *Acta Apostolicae Sedis,* XIV, p. 460.

[9] Vermeersch-Creusen, *Epitome Iur. Can.,* I, p. 137, No. 207.

[10] Canon 488: 7.

[11] Canon 488: 1.

[12] *Epitome Iur. Can.,* III, p. 116, No. 261.

ever, before absolution is granted a member of anti-social societies, one of the conditions to be fulfilled is at least seriously to promise to denounce all clerics and religious known to be members to the Holy Office.[13]

It is well that a religious superior remember that he cannot interfere with a subject about to denounce a cleric or religious he knows to be an anti-social sectary.[14]

While it is hardly likely that a cleric or religious would in these days ally himself to Freemasonry, or a kindred sect, yet it is evident that the Church has had some good reason for making the law of paragraph 2 of Canon 2336.

[13] Cf. Pagella S. Poen., apud Hilling, *C. I. C. Supplementum,* p. 51.

[14] Canon 501 : 2.

CHAPTER V

THOSE PUBLICLY KNOWN AS MEMBERS OF ANTI-SOCIAL
SOCIETIES CANNOT RECEIVE CHRISTIAN BURIAL AND
ARE DEPRIVED OF OTHER PUBLIC FUNERAL OFFICES
OF THE CHURCH. CANONS 1240; 1 AND 1241.

1240: 1 ECCLESIASTICA SEPULTURA PRIVANTUR NISI ANTE
MORTEM ALIQUA DEDERINT POENITENTIAE SIGNA . . . SECTAE
MASSONICAE ALIISVE EIUSDEM GENERIS SOCIETATIBUS NOTORIE
ADDICTI.

1241. EXCLUSO AB ECCLESIASTICA SEPULTURA DENEGANDA
QUOQUE QUAELIBET MISSA EXEQUIALIS, ETIAM ANNIVERSARIA,
TUM ALIA PUBLICA OFFICIA FUNEBRIA.

CHRISTIAN burial is the honor the Church pays those of
her children who die in her communion, and can never be
claimed for one who lived and died outside her fold. Before
the codification, it was the law that if an excommunicate was
buried in consecrated ground, the place was thereby dese-
crated and the remains had to be exhumed, if possible, and
buried elsewhere.[1] Even in the new law, " *excommunicati
vitandi* are to be exhumed, if buried in consecrated ground,[2]
if this can be done without great inconvenience, and the
church [3] or cemetery in which a person excommunicated by a
declaratory or damnatory sentence is buried is thereby violated.[4]

[1] Cf. C. 12 in X, de sepulturis, III, 28.
[2] Canon 1242.
[3] Canon 1172: 1: 1.
[4] Canon 1207.

78

Concerning the burial of Freemasons, many questions were debated in the beginning of the last century. The Holy Office, December 1, 1840, in response to a petition, declared that the anniversaries of Masons who died after receiving of the last sacraments might be celebrated, and that the corpses of the same could receive ecclesiastical burial. If the emblems of the sect had been placed on the remains at the unretracted request of the deceased made after he had received absolution, the body could not receive Christian burial for the Mason had died impenitent. If they had been placed on the corpse against the will of the deceased, the body could be given ecclesiastical burial on condition that the emblems were removed as soon as noticed, and before the body was placed in state.[5]

It was also declared, in the instruction of the Holy Office, to the Vicar Apostolic of Port-Louis, that if a body was brought to the lodge for Masonic services in compliance with the unretracted wish of the deceased, it could not receive Christian sepulture; if against his will, the deceased was not to be deprived of ecclesiastical burial. If he had died without absolution, but had evinced some signs of penance, he might be absolved after death, and his body buried with the rites of the Church.[6]

Some years later, in the instruction " Pestis Massonismi ", addressed to the Brazilian Hierarchy by the Holy Office, July 2, 1878, outlining the mode of procedure to be followed by the Brazilian clergy in dealing with the members of the Masonic sect, it was stated that they were to be denied ecclesiastical sepulture, unless they repented their sins, were absolved, and thus reconciled to the Church. If however, for some good reason, a dying Mason could not obtain absolu-

[5] C. I. C. Fontes, IV, p. 164, No. 884.
[6] C. I. C. Fontes, IV, p. 206, No. 932.

tion, but nevertheless gave some signs of sorrow,[7] he could be buried in consecrated ground, but without pomp and ceremony.[8]

This brief historical outline brings the question down to the legislation of the Code.

Ecclesiastical sepulture is understood as meaning the transfer of the body of the deceased to the church, the funeral rites celebrated over it there, and the interment in a place legitimately deputed for the burying of the faithful.[9] Such a place is a cemetery blessed with either the solemn [10] or simple blessing [11] according to the proper rite in the liturgical books.[12]

To exclude a member of an anti-social society from ecclesiastical sepulture, his membership would have to be publicly known, i. e. " notorie addicti ".　Wernz says that a fact is *notorium* if the evidence is so certain that it cannot be hidden in any way,[13] and the law of the Code makes a fact *notorium* when it is publicly known and in such circumstances that it cannot be concealed.[14]　Membership might also have notoriety of law; the Ordinary, for some good reason, might see fit to declare by a declaratory sentence that a certain individual incurred the censure of canon 2335.[15] However, it would matter little, whether the membership became publicly known before or after the member's death.[16]

---

[7] Cf. Fagnanus, 28, de sepult., No. 12-13, Ferraris, s. v. " Excommunicatio ", V.

[8] *C. I. C. Fontes,* IV, p. 377, No. 1056.

[9] Canon 1204.

[10] Cf. *Pontificale Romanum,* II, de coem. bene.

[11] *Rituale Romanum,* VIII, c. 20.

[12] Canon 1205: 1.

[13] *Ius Decretalium,* VI, No. 17.

[14] Canon 2197: 3.

[15] Canon 2223 and 2197: 2.

[16] A Coronata, *De Locis et Temporibus Sacris,* p. 265, No, 258.

If a publicly known member of these societies should have given some signs of repentance before death, he is not deprived of Christian burial. What these signs are can be learned, as the Holy Office pointed out, from approved authors.[17] They would be any act of piety, the striking of the breast, the kissing of a crucifix, an ejaculation, or the like.

Those excluded from ecclesiastical burial are also to be denied all funeral masses, or *missae exequiales*. A *Missa exequialis* is one said with the body present in the church.[18] Hence, any funeral mass, solemn, sung or merely read is forbidden by law. The term *missa exequialis* cannot be extended, as Blat thinks,[19] to include requiem masses. Although anniversary masses are forbidden, that is those celebrated yearly on the anniversary of the death of a person, nevertheless there is no prohibition of having a mass, and even a requiem mass, when the calendar permits, said privately for a deceased Mason.[20]

Other public funeral offices would be the liturgical offices attendant upon the burial of the faithful, all the ceremonies of the ritual, and even the Office of the Dead. However, private prayers can be said for a deceased anti-social sectary, even though public prayers are forbidden.[21]

Those who dare command or coerce the ecclesiastical authorities to grant Christian burial to a Mason who died impenitent, incur *ipso facto* excommunication *nemini reservatam*.[22] In the case where the authorities prudently judge

[17] Cf. Fagnanus, 28 de sepult. No. 12-13; Ferraris, s. v. "Excommunicatio", V.

[18] A Coronata, *De Locis et Temporibus Sacris,* p. 238, No. 235.

[19] *Com. Cod. Iur. Can.,* III; 2, p. 121, n. 101.

[20] Cf. Noldin, *Sum. Theo. Mor.,* III, p. 201, Genicot-Salsmans, *Inst. Theo. Mor.,* II, p. 195, No. 221.

[21] Canon 2262: 2: 1.

[22] Canon 2339.

grave harm will be done either religion or themselves, if they refuse ecclesiastical burial to a deceased Mason, they may grant it, as long as it will not be construed as in contempt of religion; this is after all only an ecclesiastical law, and cannot bind under such grave inconveniences.[23]

[23] Oietti, *Syn. Rer. Mor. et Iur. Pont.*, No. 3704.

CHAPTER VI

BOOKS DEFENDING ANTI-SOCIAL SOCIETIES CONDEMNED IPSO JURE

CANONS 1399: 8 AND 2318: 1

CANON 1399: 8.

IPSO IURE PROHIBENTUR:—

8. LIBRI . . . QUI DE SECTIS MASSONICIS VEL ALIIS EIUSDEM GENERIS SOCIETATIBUS AGENTES, EAS UTILES ET NON PERNICIOSAS ECCLESIAE ET CIVILI SOCIETATI ESSE CONTENDUNT.

CANON 2318: 1.

1. IN EXCOMMUNICATIONEM SEDI APOSTOLICAE SPECIALI MODO RESERVATAM IPSO FACTO INCURRUNT, OPERE PUBLICI IURIS FACTO, EDITORES LIBRORUM APOSTATARUM, HAERETICORUM ET SCHISMATICORUM, QUI APOSTASIAM, HAERESIM, SCHISMA PROPUGNANT, ITEMQUE EOSDEM LIBROS ALIOSVE PER APOSTOLICAS LITTERAS NOMINATIM PROHIBITOS DEFENDENTES AUT SCIENTER SINE DEBITA LICENTIA LEGENTES VEL RETINENTES.

PIUS VII in the Apostolic Constitution " Ecclesiam ",[1] Sept. 13, 1821 condemned the books, writings and other literature of the Carbonari,—" catechismos, et libros, quibus a ' Carbonariis ' describuntur quae in eorum conventibus geri solent: eorum etiam statuta, codices, ac libros omnes ad eorum defensionem exaratos, sive typis editos sive manuscriptos ". He forbade anyone to read or keep these books in his possession, also under pain of excommunication, reserved to the Holy See, and he further ordained that these

---

[1] C. I. C. Fontes, II, p. 721, No. 479; Bull. Rom. Cont., XV, p. 446.

83

books be turned over to the Ordinary or other competent ecclesiastic.

The Holy Office, February 1, 1871, called the attention of the Vicar Apostolic of Mysore in India to this condemnation of the books and writings of the Carbonari, applying it also to those of the Masons. In a previous communication the Vicar Apostolic related how he ordered the writings, diplomas of admission, and other instruments of the Masons and Carbonari should be brought to the priest and burned. It was dangerous, he said, to preserve them. The Holy Office [2] however, whilst considering this procedure sufficiently prudent, instructed the Vicar that, nevertheless, when such writings were delivered to the priest that the Church or State had reason to know about, the prescription of the constitution " Ecclesiam " was to be followed, if possible, i. e., that they be delivered to the Ordinary or others competent to receive them.[3]

Some time later, January 25, 1897, Pope Leo XIII, cognizant of the danger to faith and morals from bad and pernicious books, issued a constitution, by name " Officiorum ac Munerum ",[4] promulgating certain General Decrees about the Prohibition and Censorship of books, in which is found the following regulation:—

Prohibentur pariter libri . . . qui de sectis massonicis, vel aliis eiusdem generis societatibus agunt, easque utiles et non perniciosas Ecclesiae et civili societati esse contendunt.[5]

As can be seen from a comparison with Canon 1399: 8 as quoted above, they are almost identical, the only difference

[2] *C. I. C. Fontes*, IV, p. 319, No. 1014.

[3] *C. I. C. Fontes*, II, p. 724, No. 479, paragraph 11.

[4] *C. I. C. Fontes*, III, p. 502, No. 632; *Leonis XIII Acta*, XVIII, p. 17.

[5] *C. I. C. Fontes*, III, No. 632, p. 507, *Decreta Generalia*, etc, cap. V, n. 14.

being in the words *agunt* and *agentes*, of which more below.

By the Code the following are among those prohibited *ipso iure*: all books written of the Masons or other societies of the same nature, which contend that these societies are useful and not obnoxious to the Church or State.[6] Vermeersch says that the treatment should be such that it constitutes a real argument, although not the only argument in the work, or treatise, and that it is not enough that the utility and harmlessness of these societies to the Church and State be referred to only in passing.[7] The contending should be "non sine vi",—literally, of course, for "*contendere enim est vehementer affirmare*".[8]

It will be noticed that the *agunt* of "Officiorum ac Munerum", No. 14 has become *agentes* in Canon 1399: 8. Does it not appear that this was placed in the present participle to denote that the mere treating of the Freemasons and similar societies, and their society affairs, do not mark a book or work as prohibited, but that the treatment should be such as argues for their utility and harmlessness?

And does the Censure of Canon 2318: 1 apply to books concerning condemned societies? *Per se* no. It is obvious from the sense of Canon 2318: 1 and from a comparison of the Constitution, "Officiorum ac Munerum", with the Code on this question, that there is *no excommunication,* for the reading or retaining of such books.

This is of course not true if the books *de secta massonica aliisve eiusdem generis societatibus* have been condemned *per apostolicas litteras nominatim*.[9]

---

[6] Cf. Canon 2335.

[7] Vermeersch, *De Prohibitione et Censura Librorum,* ed. 2, p. 62.

[8] Ibid.

[9] Cfr. Canon 2318: 1.

CHAPTER VII

MEMBERS OF SECRET SOCIETIES AND THE RIGHT OF PATRONAGE

CANON 1453: 1 AND 3.

1. IUS PATRONATUS PERSONALE TRANSMITTI VALIDE NEQUIT AD ADSCRIPTOS SOCIETATIBUS SECRETIS AB ECCLESIA DAMNATIS.

3. SI RES, CUI IUS PATRONATUS REALE COHAERET, AD ALI- QUAM PERSONAM DE QUA IN § 1 TRANSEAT, IUS PATRONATUS SUSPENSUM MANET.

Ius patronatus is defined as the "summa privilegiorum cum quibusdam oneribus quae ex Ecclesiae concessione competunt fundatoribus catholicae ecclesiae, cappellae aut beneficii, vel etiam eis qui ab illis causam habent".[1] Personal right of patronage is that which directly belongs to the person,[2] while real *juspatronatus* is that which is connected with some property, and is enjoyed by the person owning the property. From the time of the Code's going into effect, no *juspatronatus* can be validly erected under any pretext.[3] For the valid transfer of the personal juspatronatus, the consent of the Ordinary in writing is required, "salvis legibus fundationis itemque praescripto can. 1470, § 1, n. 4.[4] Canon 1470, § 1 n. 4 provides that the right of patronage, if the family, clan, or line to which it is reserved by the foundation, dies out, the right also dies, does not be-

[1] Can. 1448.
[2] Canon 1449: 1.
[3] Canon 1450: 1.
[4] Canon 1453: 2.

86

come hereditary, and the Ordinary cannot validly permit the giving of the right to another.

The explicit mention made in this Canon (1453) of persons members of condemned secret societies would seem to be entirely new in law. Prior to the Code all excommunicated, whether *tolerati* or *vitandi,* were excluded from the juspatronatus.[5] Gregory IX, who reigned from 1227 to 1241,[6] ruled regarding those excommunicated :—

Ipso iure rescriptum, vel processus per ipsum habitus, non valeat, si ab excommunicato super alio quam excommunicationis vel appellationis articulo fuerit impetratum.[7]

By reason of which regulation it was held that excommunicates *tolerati* and *vitandi* could not validly receive the *juspatronatus.* Some writers thought that the Constitution of Martin V, " Ad Evitanda," [8] had ameliorated the condition of excommunicates " quoad gratias recipiendas," but Wernz points out that it did not : " Denique inhabiles quoque ad ' acquirendum ' juspatronatum sunt apostatae, haeretici, schismatici, excommunicati sive ' vitandi ' sive ' tolerati ', quorum conditio quoad gratias ecclesiasticas recipiendas a Martino V. non facta est melior." [9] Aichner held that excommunicates could acquire the *juspatronatus* but only *habitu,* not *actu,*[10] which he explains in a footnote " extruendo ecclesiam de consensu episcopi, etiamsi hoc admitti non debeat."

Since the interest here is only with the inhability of members of condemned secret societies, the above brief history is sufficient for an understanding of Canon 1453.

[5] Vermeersch-Creusen, *Epitome Iur. Can.,* II, p. 452, No. 782.

[6] Ott, " Gregory IX," *Cath. Ency.,* VI, 799.

[7] *C. I. C. de Rescriptis,* III, No. 510.

[8] *C. I. C. Fontes,* I, p. 58, No. 45.

[9] Wernz, *Ius Decretalium,* tom. II, pars 2a, pp. 170-171, No. 409.

[10] Aichner, *Compendium Iuris Eccl.,* ed. 6a, p. 308, No. 90.

By the new Code the members of condemned secret societies are singled out together with apostates, heretics, schismatics, and "excommunicati post sententiam declaratoriam aut condemnatoriam."

Adscripti are those persons actually members. *Societates secretae* are certainly those societies that demand an oath of secrecy, or of blind obedience to occult or unknown leaders.[11] Blat thinks that the term means societies that are secret *saltem quoad praxes*.[12] Besides the Freemasons, who are not only anti-social but also secret, and the Odd Fellows, the Knights of Pythias, the Sons of Temperance, and the Independent Order of Good Templars, the only other societies that would come under this heading are those mentioned above, "quae a sectatoribus secretum nemini pandendum et omnimodam obedientiam occultis ducibus praestandum iure iurando exigunt."

Damnatae; societies may be condemned by name, or " in genere, vel singulariter vel inter alias comprehensis ".[13]

The determining factor of this canon is that the societies must be secret. A personal *juspatronatus* cannot be transferred validly to a member of a condemned secret society. A real *juspatronatus* transferred to a member of a condemned secret society is said, not to cease, but to be suspended. The transfer is valid, but the one receiving it because of his disability cannot exercise it. If he quit the condemned secret society, or if the right of patronage be transferred to one not *inhabilis,* it can be validly exercised.[14]

---

[11] *C. I. C. Fontes,* IV, p. 415, No. 1085, par. 4:

[12] Blat., *Com. Cod. Iur. Can.,* III, 2, p. 440, No. 357.

[13] Blat., *Com. Cod. Iur. Can.,* III, 2, p. 440, No. 331.

[14] Cf. Augustine, *Commentary,* VI, p. 527.

CHAPTER VIII

DISABILITIES OF MEMBERS OF CONDEMNED SOCIETIES

ARTICLE I. ADMISSION TO ASSOCIATIONS OF THE FAITHFUL INVALID

CANON 693: 1.

. . . ET DAMNATAE SECTAE ADSCRIPTI . . . . VALIDE RECIPI NEQUEUNT (IN PIIS FIDELIUM ASSOCIATIONIBUS).

THIS canon, drawn originally from the Epistle " Quamquam Dolores " and the Constitution " Exortae ",[1] the one addressed to Msgr. Vital Maria Gonsalves Oliveira, the other to all the Bishops of Brazil, was brought about by the long persecution the Church and the faithful suffered at the hands of MASONIC MEMBERS OF CONFRATERNITIES AND THIRD ORDERS.

For many years prior to the great Masonic persecution of the Church in Brazil, it was only with the greatest difficulty that a person not a Mason could join a confraternity, e. g., of Mount Carmel, or the Third Order of St. Francis. By confraternity was meant much more than the pious association we know. They were sometimes bodies that had been established by Pombal for the administration of the temporalities of the parishes in order to diminish the power and authority of the Ordinaries. They handled all the parish funds, conducted, or, rather, directed the divine services, invited whom they pleased to assist at these services whether

[1] C. I. C. Fontes, III, p. 70, No. 563; C. I. C. Fontes, II, p. 99, No. 571.

89

worthy or not, and wore a special habit, and in it attended all marriages, funerals, and the like.

Annoyed at the outrages these Masonic *Confratres* and Tertiaries were perpetrating, Msgr. Gonsalves Oliveira, Bishop of Olinda, sent a circular letter to his clergy calling on them to demand that the Masonic members of the pious associations either quit their lodges, or quit the confraternities. Those chapels that pertained to the Masonic confraternities were interdicted, but, to the joy of the Masons, they continued to hold services in their Masonic regalia. The Bishop of Para, Msgr. Maçedo, had issued a like ordination. The affair went so far that the parish priests of Olinda and Para were notified that if the Masonic confraternity-members were not permitted to appear in church and receive, in their Masonic capacity, the Holy Eucharist, the confraternities would remove the sacred vessels and take possession of the tabernacle keys. They shortly did so, and the priests were forced to beg them for the keys every time they had to go on a sick call. Olinda and Para were without Holy Mass. To force the interdict the Masonic Catholics (?) even invoked the aid of the civil authority, which, by imperial edict, commanded the Bishops to lift the interdict against the confraternities. At this juncture Pius IX wrote the Epistle " Quamquam Dolores ".[2] In " Quamquam Dolores " Pius IX approved all that had been done by Msgrs. Oliveira and Maçedo, and the Pontiff benignly suspended for a year the reservation of the censure of " Apostolicae Sedis ",[3] and empowered any confessor approved by the local Ordinary to absolve from it. Furthermore Msgr. Oliveira was given the faculty of proceeding according to the severity of Canon Law against spiritual sodalities which had been warring against

[2] *C. I. C. Fontes*, III, p. 70, No. 563; Cf. Parsons, Reuben, in *Amer. Cath. Quar. Review*, XXIII, p. 808, seq.

[3] *C. I. C. Fontes*, III, p. 27, No. 552, II, 4.

the Church, of dissolving them and of erecting others. The Holy Father concluded by commanding that the letter be communicated to all Brazilian Bishops.[4]

A fortnight after " Quamquam Dolores " was promulgated, and, in those days, some months before it arrived in Brazil, Don Pedro commanded by imperial edict that the Episcopate withdraw the interdict under which the confraternities labored. He claimed that since the condemnation of Freemasonry had never received the imperial *exequatur,* the Freemasons could not be interdicted. It seems more than a mere coincidence that the imperial edict and the Apostolic Letter came to the hands of Msgr. Oliveira at the same moment. The Bishop therefore wrote the Emperor that he received both the imperial commands and the Pontifical approval of all that he had done against the Masonic confraternities, and he gave as his answer to the dilemma : " Your majesty shall judge whether I am free to obey your commands." [5]

What happened on the heels of this can be told in a word : the two prelates, Msgrs. Oliveira and Maçedo, after having been shamefully abused, were given a farce-trial, and unjustly condemned to four years of hard labor. *His Gracious Majesty,* Don Pedro, exempted them from hard labor and reduced the four-year sentence to two years. This in 1875.

There have always been some who claim exemption, for some reason, or other, from the general laws of the Church. The Masons in Brazil were of this number, and they claimed, as did Don Pedro, that the Apostolic condemnation of their craft did not obtain in Brazil since it lacked the imperial *placet.* Pius IX in his Encyclical " Etsi Multa ",[6] refuted

---

[4] *C. I. C. Fontes, III,* p. 70, No. 563; also in *Acta Pii Noni,* VI, p. 182.

[5] Parsons, Reuben, in *Amer. Cath. Quar. Review,* XXIII, p. 812.

[6] *C. I. C. Fontes,* III, No. 566, p. 86, paragraph 20.

this error, and again, in the epistle " Exortae ", with direct reference to the false claims of Don Pedro and the Brazilian Masons, the Pontiff declared :—

Atque ediximus in Constitutionibus non unos percelli Massonicos coetus in Europa constitutos, sed omnes quotquot in America aliisque totius orbis plagis habentur.[7]

In this epistle Pius IX said that he could not but wonder that when the interdicts against the churches and sodalities (i. e. of Masonic confraternities) had been lifted by His Apostolic Authority, this was made an occasion of disseminating the falsehood that the condemnation of Freemasonry had been lifted for the Masons of Brazil, and that consequently they could be admitted once more to the confraternities.

How far from the truth this was is easily seen from the above declarations, and also from a letter the Pontiff had written to Don Pedro. The Holy Father had promised to withdraw the interdict when Bishops Maçedo and Oliveira were released from prison, and when the Masonic members were removed from the offices they held in the sodalities. He could have had no other purpose than that of giving the Imperial Government the opportunity of restoring the societies to their original status, and of enabling the Freemasons to quit their evil way and return to the Church. And he took another occasion to lay all doubt, or error, that the Masonic societies in Brazil or anywhere else on earth, were exempted from the condemnation and censure against their sect in the Apostolic Constitutions.[8] This brings the legislation down to the Code.

With regard to Canon 693 : 1, most writers repeat the very

[7] C. I. C. Fontes, III, p. 99, No. 571; Acta Pii Noni, VI, p. 210.
[8] C. I. C. Fontes, III, p. 100, No. 571.

words of the law without a word of explanation.[9] *Damnatae sectae adscripti* seems to signify all those actually members of any condemned society.[10] These persons cannot be validly admitted to associations of the faithful, namely:

Associationes distinctae a religionibus vel societatibus de quibus in can. 487-681 ab Ecclesia constitui possunt vel ad perfectiorem vitam christianam inter socios promovendam, vel ad aliqua pietatis aut caritatis opera exercenda, vel deinque ad incrementum publici cultus.[11]

These societies are: Third Orders Secular, Confraternities and Pious Unions.[12] Third Orders Secular are aggregations of secular tertiaries, who being in the world strive towards Christian perfection under the guidance of some order and according to its spirit.[13] Associations of the faithful erected for the exercise of works of piety or charity are called pious unions.[14] If pious unions are constituted after the manner of organized bodies they are called sodalities. Sodalities erected for the increase of public worship, e. g., the Children of Mary, Priests' and People's, the Eucharistic League, are known under the specific name of confraternities.[15]

As a consequence of the invalid admission of a member of a condemned society to an association of the faithful, he, of course, cannot enjoy the rights and privileges of the lawful members.

---

[9] Cf. Vermeersch-Creusen, *Epitome Iur. Can.*, I, p. 471, No. 791; Augustine, *Commentary*, III, p. 435; Cocchi, II, p. 325, No. 178; Blat, II, p. 735, No. 772.

[10] Cf. Chapter on Canon 1065: 1.

[11] Canon 685.

[12] Canon 700.

[13] Canon 702: 1.

[14] Canon 701: 1.

[15] Canon 707: 2.

ARTICLE II

MARRIAGE WITH CATHOLICS

CANON 1065.

1. ABSTERREANTUR QUOQUE FIDELES A MATRIMONIO CON-
TRAHENDO CUM IIS QUI NOTORIE AUT CATHOLICAM FIDEM
ABIECERUNT, ETSI AD SECTAM ACATHOLICAM NON TRANSIERINT,
AUT SOCIETATIBUS AB ECCLESIA DAMNATIS ADSCRIPTI SUNT.

2. PAROCHUS PRAEDICTIS NUPTIIS NE ASSISTAT, NISI CON-
SULTO ORDINARIO, QUI, INSPECTIS OMNIBUS REI ADIUNCTIS, EI
PERMITTERE POTERIT UT MATRIMONIO INTERSIT, DUMMODO
URGEAT GRAVIS CAUSA ET PRO SUO PRUDENTI ARBITRIO ORDIN-
ARIUS IUDICET SATIS CAUTUM ESSE CATHOLICAE EDUCATIONI
UNIVERSAE PROLIS ET REMOTIONI PERICULI PERVERSIONIS
ALTERIUS CONIUGIS.

MATRIMONY as contracted between two baptized persons
is a sacrament, instituted by our Blessed Lord.[1] It is, moreover, a sacrament of the living, for it presupposes grace in
those who receive it. It cannot, therefore, be lawfully received by one not in the state of grace.[2] Matrimony, unlike
other sacraments, is synchronically conferred and received:
the spouses are both ministers and subjects of the sacrament.[3]
For this reason it was at one time taught that one who mar-
ried in mortal sin committed two sins, one for receiving a
sacrament unworthily, another for conferring a sacrament in
the same condition.[4] Although this opinion is no longer
commonly held, it led to what the older Canonists called the
impediment of unworthiness.[5]

[1] *Conc. Trident.*, sess. VII, de sacramentis in genere, can. 1.

[2] Ferreres, *Com. Theo. Mor.*, II, p. 177, No. 297.

[3] Liguori, *Theo. Mor.*, VI, No. 897.

[4] Liguori, *Theo. Mor.*, VI, No. 32.

[5] Cf. Gasparri, *De Matrimonio*, I, p. 326, No. 476; de Becker, *De Spon.
et Mat.*, II, p. 251.

The interest here is, of course, only with unworthiness relative to members of condemned societies, which is *indignitas ratione censurae* or *indignitas ratione peccati*, depending on whether or not the society to which the unworthy person belonged was condemned under censure, or only under grave sin.

The history of this kind of unworthiness is rather interesting. The first mention of it in law is found in the famous instruction of the Holy Office to the Vicar Apostolic of Port-Louis, August 1, 1855. It seems the Vicar had commanded his priests to treat Catholics who had joined the Masons, but refused to leave their sect, as Protestants in regard to marriage with Catholics, and the said marriages as mixed marriages. The Holy Office can hardly be said to have approved this method of treatment. If anything, it disapproved of it, and pointed out to the worthy Prelate that as yet no general decree on the question had been given. It went on to say that great prudence had to be used in cases of the kind, and that no general rule could be laid down. Catholics were, however, to be dissuaded from entering such marriage, if this could be done quietly and without scandal. But, since to refuse to perform marriages of this nature would lead to many entering into lives of sin, the Vicar Apostolic was instructed to decide in each case what his prudence dictated.[6]

Six years later, the Vicar Apostolic of Marysville, in the United States, asked the Holy Office if it were licit to assist at the marriage of those who were, not only Protestants, but also Masons, when marrying Catholics, and also if it were permitted to assist at the marriage of a Catholic who had joined the Masons. The Holy Office answered, August 21, 1861, that at such marriages the pastors were to conduct

---

[6] *C. I. C. Fontes*, IV, p. 206, No. 932.

themselves as at the marriages of public sinners.   Continuing, the response repeated, almost word for word, what had
been said on the matter to the Vicar Apostolic of Port-Louis,
August 1, 1855, seen above.[7]

June 28, 1865 the Holy Office again answered that the
Ordinary was to decide what he thought best, " dummodo
absit scandalum ", with regard to marriages of Catholics
with Masons.[8]   When, some two years later, the same
Congregation was asked what if a Mason asked to be mar-
ried by the Church only to satisfy the desire of the bride, it
repeated the above decree.[9]

The first definite legislation about these marriages was
outlined in the instruction of the Holy Office to the Bishops
of Brazil.   Marriages of Catholics and Masons were to be
performed, stripped of all religious rites and ceremonies.
When a Mason asked to marry a Catholic, the pastor was to
try to convert him and persuade him to quit his lodge.   If he
refused to do so, the fiancee and her parents were to be exhorted to withdraw their assent to the matrimonial agreement.   If this was also refused, and the priest prudently believed that if he did not assist at the purposed marriage
grave harm or scandal would ensue, he was to consult the
Ordinary, who received by the instruction the faculty of
permitting passive assistance to all such marriages.   No
blessing, or other ceremony could be given, not to speak of a
Nuptual Mass.   The pastor was to assist only as the Church's
authorized witness, and even his assistance was granted only
under condition that the Catholic faith and education of all
offspring of the marriage was properly safeguarded.[10]

[7] C. I. C. Fontes, IV, pp. 239-240, No. 967.

[8] Collectanea S. C. P. F., II, p. 1, No. 1300.

[9] Ibid.

[10] C. I. C. Fontes, IV, p. 377, No. 1056.

In other parts of the world the Masonic oath, when unretracted, came to be looked upon as constituting an impediment to matrimony, of even a greater degree than heresy. The argument was this: the teaching of Freemasonry was not only heretical, but also anti-Christian, and its ultimate purpose was the uprooting of all faith and the overturning of the Church. Why then should heretics who, at least, believed in Christ and the Triune God, be barred from marriage with Catholics, if those banded together for the destruction of Christianity and whose secret conspiracies were causing revolutions all over Europe, were not? [11]

With this as a premise, the Vicar Apostolic of Bombay asked the Holy Office if this oath could, or should, be treated as a matrimonial impediment, either diriment or impedient, and what promises should be demanded in order that pastors might validly and licitly assist at the marriage of a Catholic to one who had taken the Masonic oath. The Holy Office answered, February 21, 1883, in almost the same tenor as in the five previous decrees. However, the word *notorie* was introduced in the phrase *adscripti sectae massonicae,* and Mass was allowed if conditions or circumstances demanded it. Regarding the question of pre-marriage promises, nothing was said.[12]

As has already been briefly touched, some of the pre-Code canonists considered the fact that one was a Mason to be a real matrimonial impediment: for example, the Vicar Apostolic of Bombay was uncertain whether it was a diriment, or an impedient impediment.[13] De Becker thought that, since the Divine law demanded the state of grace for the reception of the sacrament, the state of mortal sin constituted a real

---

[11] Supplement to the *Tablet,* June 25, 1865, vol. 65, p. 1009, *et seq.*

[12] *C. I. C. Fontes,* IV, p. 412, No. 1080.

[13] Cf. S. C. S. Off., 21 Feb., 1883, *C. I. C. Fontes,* IV, No. 1080.

impediment for the one in sin, not however, for the other party who could not abstain from contracting marriage *absque gravi incommodo*,[14] Gasparri calls unworthiness an impediment " verum et proprie dictum ",[15] and Petrovits, after the Code, also considers unworthiness to be such, remarking that it is " contracted between a practical Catholic and a Catholic who is stigmatized on account of any of the foregoing three reasons ", namely public rejection of the Catholic faith, profession of membership in societies condemned by the Church, and public crime, or censure.[16]

Now, De Becker defines a matrimonial impediment as a " defectus requisitae conditionis pro celebratione matrimonii." An impediment, he says, is diriment, " si defectus talis est, ut reddat celebrationem matrimonii nullam et irritam; " impedient, " si vero defectus talis est, ut matrimonium valide contrahatur, sed eius celebratio illicita reddatur." [17] He shows, in this last definition, that by *celebratio* he means *celebratio contractus*. The *contractio* he calls valid, the *celebratio* illicit. Gasparri, however, defines an impediment as a " circumstantia quae ex lege vel divina vel humana arcet a nuptiis seu licite seu valide contrahendis," and d'Annibale,—" sunt autem impedimenta conditiones vel circumstantiae iure constitutae quae arcent a nuptiis, seu licite, seu valide contrahendis."[18]

An impediment, as such, is not defined by the Code, yet from Canon 1036 it can be learned that an impediment directly affects marriage as a contract. An impedient impediment contains a grave prohibition of contracting marriage,

---

14 De Becker, *De Spon. et Mat.*, II, p. 251.

15 Gasparri, *De Matrimonio*, I, p. 326, No. 474.

16 *The New Church Law on Matrimony*, 2nd ed., p. 124, No. 199.

17 *De Spon. et Mat.*, pp. 49-50.

18 Gasparri, *De Matrimonio*, I, p. 160, No. 255; d'Annibale, *Summula Theo. Mor.*, III, p. 336, No. 428.

which, however, does not render the marriage void, if contracted despite the impediment. A diriment impediment
both gravely prohibits the contracting of marriage, and makes
it null and void. It is clear that a matrimonial impediment
directly affects marriage, as has been said above, as a contract,
and only indirectly as a sacrament. That is, the sacrament
of matrimony is unlawfully or invalidly received, because the
matrimonial contract is illicit, or invalid.[19]   Hence, well can
Vermeersch-Creusen define an impediment as a " circumstantia quae ex iure divino in lege ecclesiastica proposito aut
ex iure mere ecclesiastico personas a contractu matrimoniali
arcet."[20]

Unworthiness is akin to mortal sin, in fact is founded on
it. Mortal sin itself does not impede the receiving of the
Sacrament of Matrimony. It is an *obex*, however, to the
receiving of the grace of the sacrament, and, when removed,
the grace is said to revivify, not because the sacrament is
received on being restored to grace, but because the sacrament was received in sin which merely suspended the grace
of the sacrament.[21]   Hence, unworthiness does not affect,
at least directly, the matrimonial contract, but rather places
an *obex* to the receiving of the sacramental grace, and this
only for the party in mortal sin. Since it is clear from Canon
1036 that matrimonial impediments affect directly the contract of marriage, and since unworthiness merely suspends
the effects of the sacrament, it remains that unworthiness is
not a canonical impediment. Moreover, impediments are removed by dispensation, but no dispensation could remove
unworthiness.[22]

[19] Cf. Canon 1012: 182.

[20] *Epitome Iur. Can.*, ed. 2a, II, p. 173, No. 176.

[21] Cf. Pesch, *Compendium Theo. Dog.*, IV, p. 27, No. 29.

[22] Wernz-Vidal, *Ius Canonicum*, V, p. 221, No. 200.

Of the writers before the Code, Wernz,[23] Sabetti,[24] de Smet,[25] and Marc,[26] negatively, at least, do not consider unworthiness an impediment. De Smet, in fact, points out that the censure, or mortal sin, under which members of condemned societies would be included, does not affect matrimony *qua contractus*.[27] And both De Becker and Gasparri who do consider unworthiness an impediment, define an impediment as a circumstance or condition affecting the liceity, or validity of matrimony as a contract. Of post-Code writers Vermeersch-Creusen,[28] Cappello,[29] Chelodi,[30] Farrugia,[31] Vlaming,[32] Genicot-Salsmans,[33] Arregui,[34] Augustine,[35] Wernz-Vidal,[36] and Schäfer,[37] do not treat unworthiness as a canonical impediment.

Unworthiness is not, therefore, an impediment, and indeed the Holy Office did not approve of the action and procedure of the Vicar Apostolic of Port-Louis, who considered unworthiness with regard to Masons as similar to the impedient impediment of Mixed Religion.[38]

[23] *Ius Decretalium*, IV, pp. 11-12.

[24] *Com. Theo. Mor.*, p. 670, No. 867.

[25] *De Spon. et Mat.*, ed. 1909, p. 895, No. 242.

[26] *Inst. Mor. Alph.*, II, p. 468, No. 1984.

[27] *De Spon. et Mat.*, p. 295, No. 242.

[28] *Epitome Iur. Can.*, ed. 2a, p. 196, No. 335: 2.

[29] *De Sacramentis*, III, p. 944.

[30] *Ius Matrimoniale*, p. 64, No. 66.

[31] *De Matrimonio*, p. 263, No. 139.

[32] *Prac. Iur. Mat.*, I, p. 215, No. 243.

[33] *Inst. Theo. Mor.*, II, p. 476, No. 509.

[34] *Sum. Theo. Mor.*, p. 593, No. 748.

[35] *Commentary*, V, p. 135.

[36] *Ius Canonicum*, V, p. 171, No. 149.

[37] *Das Eherecht nach der Codex Iuris Canonici*, p. 112.

[38] *C. I. C. Fontes*, IV, p. 206, No. 932.

The Code says that the faithful are also to be deterred from contracting marriage with members of condemned societies,—" Absterreantur quoque fideles." The old law treated only of marriage with a Mason, or a member of a similar society. The reference expressed by " quoque " is to the preceding canon, in which the Code states that it is the duty of those having the care of souls to deter the faithful from mixed marriages. Hence here in Canon 1065, the Bishops and other Pastors are also to deter the faithful from marriages with members of forbidden societies. It is their duty to do so, and it is to be done by instructing the faithful publicly, or privately of the dangers likely to follow such a marriage.[39]

It is a strange thing that it is not from marriage with all members of condemned societies, but only with those " qui *notorie* . . . societatibus ab Ecclesia damnatis adscripti sunt ". Cappello says that the term *notorie* signifies that the membership in the condemned society is " notorium notorietate facti," [40] and that it is required that the adscription to the society be publicly known. He does not, however, exclude notoriety of law, but he very well says that this will rarely be the case.[41]

Societies condemned by the Church are those condemned either by name, or implicitly, as Blat has it, " in specie " or " in genere ".[42]

Cappello included under this heading the Masons, the Carbonari, the Fenians, members of Nihilistic, Anarchistic, and " vere " Socialistic societies, members of Bible Societies, Clerico-Liberalists, Old-Catholics, members of Cremation

Societies, of the Y. M. C. A., and of all anti-social societies.[43] It is not likely that anyone would wish to contract marriage with a member of the Carbonari, the Fenians, or the Clerico-Liberalists. In the first place, all three societies are no longer extant, and the members of the last society also labored under the diriment impediment of Sacred Order, and, perhaps, of Solemn Vow.[44] The Old Catholics are rather an heretical denomination than a condemned society. The Young Men's Christian Association does not appear, as has been said, to be condemned.[45] That the Masons are condemned and other anti-social societies, such as Anarchistic and Nihilistic societies, no one will doubt. Petrovits says on the subject: " Since we treat here 'de odiosis', the terms ' societatibus ab Ecclesia damnatis adscripti sunt ' must be interpreted strictly. We would therefore conclude that this canon has in mind only members of those societies which are expressly and ' nominatim ' condemned." [46] In his enumeration he mentions the Masons, the Carbonari, the Odd Fellows, the Sons of Temperance and the Knights of Pythias.

It is sometimes asserted that societies condemned, not under censure, but only *sub gravi,* are not strictly condemned, but only prohibited. This does not seem to be absolutely true, however: Bible Societies are, without doubt, on the express declaration of the Holy See, condemned, for Gregory XVI, May 5, 1844 declared that he condemned all Bible Societies, " et cunctas societates biblicas dedum a nostris decessoribus reprobatas Apostolica rursus auctoritate con-

---

[43] *De Sacramentis,* III, p. 476, No. 330.

[44] Cf. Ency, " Quanto Conficiamur Moerere," Pii IX, 10 Augusti, 1863, para. 8; *C. I. C. Fontes,* III, p. 536, No. 973.

[45] Cf. S. C. S. Off, 5 Novembris, 1920, *Acta Apostolicae Sedis,* XII, p. 595.

[46] *The New Church Law on Matrimony,* p. 140, No. 200.

demnamus," [47] and Pius IX said that, emulating the example
of his Predecessor, Gregory XVI, he also wished that Bible
Societies be condemned.[48] Yet, they are not condemned
under censure. It is certain, also, that the three American
secret societies, the Sons of Temperance, the Knights of
Pythias, and the Odd Fellows are condemned, for they were
so termed by the Holy Office, January 19, 1896, in a response
to certain American Bishops.[49] For an equal reason, then,
the Independent Order of Good Templars is condemned.[50]
Cremation Societies affiliated to Freemasonry are also, as-
surely, condemned.[51] And if the three American secret
societies are condemned, simply because the faithful are
forbidden to join them, even though the Holy See did not
actually use the word *condemnare,* when proscribing them,
then all Cremation Societies, and all societies comprehended
in the general reprobation of societies that demand an oath
of secrecy, or blind obedience, or both, are also condemned.[52]
Hence, Petrovits is not justified in saying that only expressly
and nominally condemned societies are to be understood by
the term " societatibus ab Ecclesia damnatis " as used here.

In this canon, however, one who joined a condemned
society in good faith, and later learned of the condemnation,
but nevertheless refused to quit his society, would be considered unworthy if his membership were publicly known,
for the persons mentioned are those members of condemned
societies,—*adscripti* and not those joining,—*nomen dantes.*

---

[47] Ency. "Inter Praecipuas ", *C. I. C. Fontes,* II, p. 529, No. 803.

[48] Ency. "Qui Pluribus ", 9 Novembris, 1846, *C. I. C. Fontes,* II,
No. 504, p. 811.

[49] *Acta Sanctae Sedis,* XXVIII, p. 699.

[50] S. C. S. Off., 9 Augusti, 1893, *C. I. C. Fontes,* IV, p. 482, No. 1167.

[51] S. C. S. Off., 19 Maii, 1886, *C. I. C. Fontes,* IV, p. 428, No. 1100.

[52] Cf. S. C. S. Off., 10 Maii, 1884, *C. I. C. Fontes,* IV, p. 419, No. 1086.

The parish priest is commanded not to assist at the proposed nuptials. He cannot, therefore, of his own accord, assist at the marriage in question.[53] The prohibition affects the priest, not the parties, as if manifest from the text, and no impediment is introduced.[54] He must consult the Ordinary,—" nisi consulto Ordinario." This means, of course, the Ordinary of the Place, and includes also the Vicar General, the Vicar Capitular, and the Administrator. (Canon 198 § 1.)

All the circumstances of the case are to be weighed well by the Ordinary. It is his place to decide whether there is a sufficently grave cause to permit the marriage, and it is left to his prudent judgment also to decide whether or not the Catholic education of all the children is sufficiently safeguarded, as well as the danger of perversion to the other party. Wernz-Vidal say that it is apparent from the prescription of the law that the Ordinary is to decide these cases in the same way as he decides cases of mixed marriages.[55]

Vermeersch states, and, indeed, rightly, that the canonical reasons for asking a dispensation from an impediment are also grave causes for asking permission to assist at the marriages here treated.[56] These reasons are found in an Instruction of the Propaganda, May 9, 1877.[57] However, not only will these reasons suffice, but any other good reason: as Vlaming points out, both St. Alphonsus,[58] and Benedict XIV [59] teach that a grave injury, or loss, that might result to the innocent party, or even to the priest, or witnesses, would

---

[53] Cf. Cappello, *De Sacramentis,* III, p. 376, No. 331.

[54] Blat, *Com. Iur. Can.,* III: 2, p. 565, No. 460.

[55] Wernz-Vidal, *Ius Can.,* V, p. 222, No. 201.

[56] *Epitome Iur. Can.,* II, p. 196, No. 335.

[57] *Collectanea S. C. P. F.,* II, p. 104, No. 1470.

[58] *Theo. Mor.,* VI, No. 54.

[59] *De Synodo Dioecesana,* VIII, c. 14, No. 5.

be reason enough to permit the marriage of a Catholic to one unworthy, as also would be the scandal that might ensue, if the marriage of a Catholic to the unworthy party were not performed. In a word, whatever seems to the Ordinary reasonably grave is sufficient for him to give permission for the marriage.

Vermeersch seems to think that it is necessary that the promises be given,[60] but Cappello claims that how the Catholic education of the children and the danger of perversion of the innocent party are to be taken care of is not determined.[61] Although the Code in canon 1061 says that the Church does not dispense from the impediment of Mixed Religion, " nisi cautionem praestiterit coniux acatholicus de a coniuge catholico removendo periculo et uterque coniux de universa prole catholice tantum baptizanda et educanda," canon 1065 merely demands " dummodo cautum sit ". Hence, with Blat it can be safely said that these interests can be looked after otherwise than by demanding the promises.[62] If, on the contrary, the Ordinary saw fit to demand that the condition " cautum esse " be insured by a written agreement, it certainly seems to be within his power to demand such in writing, since the matter is left to his prudent judgment.[63]

Chelodi, acting on the pre-Code denial of any ecclesiastical rite to marriages of Catholics with unworthy Catholics, still holds that they should be celebrated " absque religioso ritu, saltem absque Missa." [64] Vlaming points out that if in mixed marriages passive assistance is no longer prescribed, but actually forbidden, since canon 1102: 1 orders that the

---

[60] Vermeersch-Creusen, *Epitome Iur. Can.*, II, p. 196, No. 335.

[61] *De Sacramentis,* III, p. 377, No. 331.

[62] *Com. Cod. Iur. Can.,* III: 1, p. 565, No. 460.

[63] Wernz-Vidal, *Ius. Can.*, V, p. 222, No. 201.

[64] *Ius Matrimoniale,* p. 64, No. 66.

interrogations concerning consent be made by the Ordinary, or pastor, so in these marriages the officiating priest is to assist actively, i. e., to ask and receive the consent of the parties.[65]   Formerly only passive assistance was allowed, as the decrees of the Holy Office of June 28, 1865,[66] January 30, 1867,[67] and January 11, 1899,[68] show.   The Code does not extend the prohibition of all sacred rites as in mixed marriages to marriages of Catholics with unworthy Catholics.[69] And although the decrees previous to the Code forbade, usually, the celebration of Mass at the marriage of Catholics with Masons, nowhere in the Code can such a prohibition be found.[70]   However, to allow Mass at such marriages would very easily cause scandal; it seems, therefore, that the Bishop, " pro suo prudenti arbitrio ", might forbid its celebration in particular instances.   As to the place of celebrating the marriages, the latest edition of the Roman Ritual make no mention of it.   According to Canon 6: 6, they can take place in Church, but again it seems that, to avoid scandal, the Bishop might command that they be celebrated elsewhere, for example, in the sacristy of the parish church, or the parlor of the parish house.[71]

It will be well to remember that unworthiness can be made an impediment by neither the Bishop,[72] nor custom.[73]

If however the Catholic party were about to marry a Mason, or a member of another condemned society, who was

[65] *Prae. Iur. Mat.*, I, p. 218, No. 280.

[66] *C. I. C. Fontes*, IV, p. 259, No. 984.

[67] *C. I. C. Fontes*, IV, p. 301, No. 998.

[68] *C. I. C. Fontes*. IV, p. 511, No. 1215.

[69] Cf. Canon 1102: 2.

[70] Cf. Vlaming, *Prae. Iur. Mat.*, I, p. 218, No. 250.

[71] Ayrinhac, *Marriage Legislation*, p. 132, No. 131.

[72] Canon 1038.

[73] Canon 1041.

also a non-Catholic, whether a baptized Protestant, or an unbaptized person, not only would the pastor be bound to consult the Ordinary before marrying the parties, but a dispensation from Mixed Religion, or Disparity of Worship, as the case might be, would also have to be obtained.[74] Canon 1109: 3 would, however, in this case apply to these marriages, and they would have to be performed outside of Church, unless the Ordinary prudently decided that the law could not be observed without great evils resulting therefrom.

ARTICLE III.   THEIR ADMISSION TO THE NOVITIATE: IS IT INVALID?

In Card. Gasparri's index to the Code, s.v., " Societates ab Ecclesia damnatae ", it is stated that " qui ad eas pertinent . . . admitti nequeunt in novitiatum ".[1]   Just what is meant by this reference is not clear.   Nowhere in the first part of this canon are the members of condemned societies said to be invalidly admitted to the novitiate, nor in the second part, illicitly.

Vermeersch-Creusen hold, and indeed rightly, that a condemned society is not, properly speaking, a non-Catholic sect.[2]   That one, a member of a condemned society is not considered a non-Catholic is shown in many places in the Code.   Canon 1065: 1 treats of the marriage of these persons with Catholics, which treatment would be unnecessary, if they were non-Catholics, for canon 1060 with its impediment of Mixed Religion would apply.[3]   Canon 1240: 1, wishing to include both those publicly known as members of non-

---

[74] S. C. S. Off., 30 Januarii, 1867, *C. I. C. Fontes*, IV, p. 301, No. 998.

[1] *Codex Iuris Canonici*, . . . ab E'mo Petro Card. Gasparri auctus, Romae, 1918, p. 775.

[2] *Epitome Iuris Canonici*, I, p. 351, No. 626.

[3] Cf. Vlaming, *Prae. Iur. Mat.*, I, p. 215, No. 244.

Catholic sects, and those publicly known as members of anti-social sects, mentions both.   On the contrary, when only one, or the other class is meant, only one or the other class is mentioned; canon 167: 1 declares ineligible to vote in canonical elections those who have joined heretical or schismatic sects, and canon 2336: 2 treats of the denunciation of clerics and religious who join anti-social societies, to be made to the Holy Office.

Furthermore, the Pontifical Commission on the Interpretation of the Code declared, October 16, 1918, that by the term " qui sectae acatholicae adhaeserunt " was meant those who, born Catholics, defected from the faith, and became members of a heretical or schismatical sect.[4]

If, however, canon 542: 1 does not render the reception of members of condemned societies into the novitiate invalid, can they be validly received?   The answer is not absolutely clear.

As has been pointed out, condemned societies considered according to the sanction attached to their condemnation may be divided into societies condemned under censure, i. e., excommunication, and societies condemned under pain of mortal sin.   There seems to be no prohibition in law forbidding the reception of persons in mortal sin into the novitiate, and therefore, members of societies condemned *sub gravi* do not appear to be received invalidly into the novitiate.   As to those who join societies condemned under censure, it appears that excommunication was considered before the Code by some as rendering the reception of excommunicates illicit,[5] and by others, invalid.[6]   The reason for these opinions was, that since excommunication removed one from communion

[4] Cf. *Acta Apostolicae Sedis,* XI, p. 477, No. 7.

[5] Cf. Suarez, *Tractatus Septimus,* V, c. 4, No. 18.

[6] Wernz, *Ius Decretalium,* III, p. 295, No. 628.

with the faithful, he could not, *iure naturali,* join a religious community.

However this might have been, excommunication in the new law has only the effects mentioned in law,[7] and nowhere can it be found that excommunicates are invalidly or illicitly admitted to the novitiate.

Let it not be said, that if members of condemned societies cannot validly be admitted to pious associations of the faithful, *a fortiori* they cannot be admitted to religious communities. What is behind the prescription of canon 693: 1 has already been seen, the outrages committed in Brazil by the Masonic members of the confraternities and sodalities. It would hardly be possible that the members of condemned societies in any large number would seek admission to religion, and the danger from such would not be as great and as imminent as the danger warded off by canon 693: 1.

Although from the common law it does not seem that the members of condemned societies are barred from reception into the novitiate, still the constitutions of a particular community could establish an impediment in the case, as, *de facto,* the constitutions of the Dominicans do.[8]

---

[7] Cf. Cappello, *De Censuris,* p. 137, No. 139; cf. also Canons 2257-2267.

[8] Constitutio 35, *Const. Sacr. Ord. Praed.,* Acta et Decreta Cap. Gen. Prov., Romae, 1924.

CHAPTER IX

Absolution and Passive Membership

ARTICLE I. ABSOLUTION.

The history of the legislation concerning absolution in the case of members of condemned societies is very involved, not to say confusing. This is due to the secrecy in which certain faculties granted to Bishops and others are wrapt, for the most part, and also to the fact that there is almost nothing to be found for nearly a hundred years after the Masons were first condemned.

There have been two occasions on which the Holy See has seen fit to relax the reservation of the censures against the members of the anti-social societies, their favorers, and the like: one is found, for the whole world, in the Constitution " Quo Graviora ";[1] the other one, for Brazil, in the Encyclical " Quamquam Dolores ".[2] These instances were really not general faculties to absolve from a papal reserved excommunication, but a relaxation of the reservation of the same.

Regarding the absolution of Masons, many questions have been presented to the Holy See for solution. Asked whether or not it was lawful to grant absolution to a Mason who, although he repented of his Masonic oath, nevertheless still communicated with his lodge and frequented its meetings, the Holy Office, July 5, 1837, answered *non licere*.[3] This

---

[1] *C. I. C. Fontes,* II, p. 733, No. 481, paragraph 19.

[2] *C. I. C. Fontes,* III, p, 71, No. 563.

[3] *Collectanea S. C. P. F.,* I, p. 498, No. 868; *C. I. C. Fontes,* IV, p. 160, No. 877.

response left something to be desired; it was unlawful, certainly, to grant absolution, but was that absolution also invalid? This further doubt the Holy Office settled about a year later by declaring that it was invalid.[4]

The celebrated letter of the Vicar Apostolic of Port-Louis to the Cardinal Prefect of the Propaganda made reference also to the absolution of Masons and asked information in the matter. The Holy Office in response repeated the above decrees of July 5, 1837, and June 27, 1838.[5]

The Bishop of St. Hyacinth, in the ecclesiastical province of Montreal, inquired of the Holy Office if those persons could be admitted to sacramental absolution who joined the Masons solely for temporal reasons, or, rather, to avoid temporal losses, "intendendo di rimanere cattolici". The Holy Office replied, March 7, 1889, that, *iuxta exposita*, these Catholics could be absolved from the censure, and admitted to the sacraments on the following conditions:—

1. reapse se serio separaverint a societatibus praedictis;
2. promittant numquam amplius fore ut sese immisceant alicui actui societatum ipsarum tum secreto tum publico, et praesertim numquam amplius se soluturos requisitam contributionem;
3. removeatur scandalum eo meliori modo quo fieri potest;
4. animo sint dispositi ad suum nomen revocandum, si et quando id facere absque gravi damno poterunt.

This response His Holiness Leo XIII approved, and the Bishop was granted faculties to absolve such persons.[6]

[4] *Collectanea S. C. P. F.*, I, p. 498, No. 868; *C. I. C. Fontes*, IV, p. 160, No. 877.

[5] *Collectanea S. C. P. F.*, I, p. 596, No. 1116; *C. I. C. Fontes*, IV, p. 206, No. 932.

[6] *Collectanea S. C. P. F.*, II, p. 182, No. 1593; *C. I. C. Fontes*, IV, p. 412, No. 1080.

The Holy See was wont to grant to certain Bishops, Vicars Apostolic and Prefects Apostolic of countries far removed from Rome, from which it would have been difficult to have recourse to the various Roman Congregations, certain *Facultates Apostolicae,* called such since they were received *a Sede Apostolica.* These faculties were really an outgrowth of the great missionary movement that sprung up in the sixteenth century. They were granted to the Bishops, not *intuitu personae,* but according to the long-established custom of the Holy See, as the distances of their several dioceses from Rome, and the good of souls necessitated.[7] Indeed the constitution " Operiosum " of the Propaganda, dated February 10, 1657, formed the preface of a new schedule of faculties that was then long in existence.[8]

Prior to the Code, these faculties, in formula I, art. 16, of the formulae usually presented to American Bishops, contained the following power :—

Absolvendi ab omnibus censuris etiam speciali modo in Bulla "Apostolicae Sedis moderationi" diei 12 Octobris, 1869, Romano Pontifici reservatis, excepta absolutione accomplicis in peccato turpi.[9]

This faculty was also enjoyed by the Bishops of Canada, England, Scotland,[10] Germany, Austria, Hungary, Poland, Belgium,[11] and by all Vicars and Prefects Apostolic.[12]   It

[7] Inst. *S. C. P. F.,* 16 Aug. 1787, *Collectanea S. C. P. F.,* vol. I, p. 330, No. 549.

[8] *Collectanea S. C. P. F.,* I, p. 25, No. 88.

[9] Cf. Konings, *Commentarium Facultates Apostolicas,* ed. 1884, p. 54, No. 73; Putzer, *Commentarium in Facultates Apostolicas,* ed. 1893, p. 193, No. 139.

[10] Putzer, *Com. in Fac. Apos.,* p. 193, No. 139.

[11] Putzer, *Com. in Fac. Apos.,* p. 371, No. 244.

[12] Putzer, *Com. in Fac. Apos.,* p. 373, No. 245.

contained, of course, the power of absolving from the censure of cap. II, n. 4, of the Constitution "Apostolicae Sedis":

Nomen dantes sectae "Massonicae" aut "Carbonariae" aut aliis ejusdem generis sectis, quae contra Ecclesiam vel legitimas potestates seu palam, seu clandestine machinantur, nec non iisdem sectis favorem qualemcunque praestantes: earumve occultos coriphaeos ac duces non denunciantes.[13]

In the Pagella granted to the Bishops of Italy prior to the Code by the Sacred Penitentiary is found the following faculty "pro foro conscientiae":—

Absolvendi a censuris, et poenis ecclesiasticis eos, qui sectis vetitis Massonicis, aut Carbonariis, aliisque similibus nomen dederunt, aut favorem praestiterunt, ita tamen ut a respectiva secta omnino separent, eamque abiurent; libros, manuscripta, ac signa sectam respicientia, si quae retineant, in manus absolventis tradant ad Ordinarium quamprimum caute transmittenda, aut saltem, si iustae gravesque causae id postulent, comburenda, iniuncta pro modo culparum gravi poenitentia salutari, cum frequentia sacramentalis confessionis, nec non absolvendi eos, qui eiusmodi sectarum duces ac magistros occultos denunciare culpabiliter neglexerint, iniuncta pariter salutari poenitentia, et firma obligatione sub reincidentia eosdem Vobis, vel aliis, ad quos spectat, prout de iure, denuntiandi.[14]

This Pagella and the above faculty were also enjoyed by the Bishops in the United States.[15]

Although this faculty was for the internal forum it could be used by the Bishop and his Vicar General "in spiritualibus", "dummodo in Sacro Presbyteratus Ordine" even

[13] *C. I. C. Fontes*, III, p. 27, No. 552.
[14] Marc, *Inst. Mor. Alphonsianae*, II, appendix I, No. 2, p. 734.
[15] Putzer, *Com. in Fac. Apos.*, p. 6.

outside of sacramental confession, and could be delegated habitually to the Canon Penitentiary and Vicars Forane, but only for sacramental confession, and, in particular circumstances, could be confessors even to confessers.

Besides the Pagella conceded to Bishops there was another " quae nonnullis Confessariis communicatur, pro foro conscientiae, et in Sacramentali Confessione ". The confessors who had received these faculties were not to make them known unless necessity or utility demanded. This Pagella contained, practically, the identical faculty contained in the Pagella granted Bishops: it specified, however, " aliisque iniunctis de iure iniungendis ".[16]

There soon arose some difficulty concerning the Pagella's faculty of absolving Masons; whether only occult, or also public Masons could be absolved, and whether the term *ut eiurent* demanded a formal and public abjuration that was to be preserved in the archives. The Holy Office accordingly declared, August 3, 1889, that the Bishops should use the faculties granted them in the Pagella, by which either the Bishops themselves, or their delegates, could absolve those who had become Masons, whether their membership were public, or occult, on condition that they left their sect, abjured or detested it in the presence of the confessor, repaired the scandal they had given as best they could, and fulfilled the other injunctions of the Pagella of the Sacred Penitentiary.[17]

Since all faculties contained in the Apostolic Faculties granted previous to the Code were abrogated, with the exception of those for the internal forum, by the decree of the Sacred Consistorial Congregation, " Proxima Sacra ", of April 25, 1918, the Bishops lost their faculty for the external forum contained in the formula I, art. 16, of the Apostolic Faculties. The Apostolic Delegates, however, have the

[16] Marc, *Inst. Mor. Alphonsianae*, tom. II, appendix I, No. 3. p. 737.
[17] *Collectanea S. C. P. F.*, vol. II, p. 372, No. 2014.

faculty of absolving from all reserved Papal censures, for
both internal and external forum, *iniunctis de iure iniungendis.*[18] The *se de iure iniungenda* for absolution
from the censure of Canon 2335 are those conditions
contained in the Pagella and confirmed by the Holy Office,
August 3, 1898,[19] with of course the changes made by the
Code.

What is of most importance here is the faculty contained
in the present Pagella of the Sacred Penitentiary, which as
has been said, agrees almost word for word with the pre-
Code Pagella, with, however, the changes necessitated by
the Code :—

Absolvendi a censuris et poenis ecclesiasticis eos qui nomen
dederint sectae massonicae aliisve eiusdem generis associationibus quae contra Ecclesiam vel legitimas civiles potestates machinantur; ita tamen ut a respectiva secta vel associatione omnino
se separent eamque abiurent; denuncient, iuxta Can. 2336: 2,
personas ecclesiasticas et religiosas, si quas eidem adscriptas
noverint, libros, manuscripta ac signa eamdem respicientia si
qua retineant, caute transmittenda aut, saltem, si iustae gravesque causae id postulent, destruenda; iniuncta pro modo culparum
gravi poenitentia saluti cum frequentatione sacramentalis confessionis et obligatione illata scandala reparandi.[20]

There are certain points of law concerning excommunication and its absolution that it would be well to call to mind
here. Censures of their very nature are of the external
forum.[21] Excommunication deprives a person of the privileges he enjoys, not as an individual, but as a member of the

[18] Hilling, *Codicis Iuris Canonici Supplementum,* p. 27, No. 4; Vermeersch-Creusen, *Epitome Iur. Can.,* I, p. 480.   Appendix I, No. 813.

[19] *Collectanea S. C. P. F.,* II, p. 372, No. 2014.

[20] Hilling, *C. I. C. Supplementum,* p. 51, Cf. with Marc, *Inst. Mor.
Alphonsianae,* II, appendix I, Nos. 2 and 3, pp. 734 and 737.

[21] D'Annibale, *Sum. Theo. Mor.,* I, pp. 332, 346, nota 14.

Church.   Hence absolution from excommunication, since it restores the rights enjoyed by a member of the ecclesiastical society, is also, of necessity, an act of the external forum. Ayrinhac well says :

There are cases when . . . because of insufficient reparation or for other reasons, the censured party cannot be readily re-admitted to full participation of the privileges of the faithful, and on the other hand the Church does not wish to deprive him any longer of certain powers or means of grace which he may urgently need.   He is then allowed the private use of these powers or means without being publicly restored to his former state.   He is absolved in the internal forum, not in the external forum.[22]

Absolution from censure granted in the external forum affects both the external and the internal forum.   One absolved in the internal forum may *remoto scandalo* be considered absolved in the external also, but unless the absolution can be proven, or may be legitimately presumed in the external forum, the censure can be enforced by proper Superiors in the external forum until absolution in that forum has also been received.[23]

A censure can be remitted only by legitimate absolution.[24] Lawful absolution from a censure can be granted by the superior who imposed the censure, his successor or superior, or one to whom the power has been conceded.[25] Absolution cannot be refused once contumacy is broken: contumacy can be said to be broken when the guilty one repents of his deed and gives, or promises sufficient satisfac-

[22] Ayrinhac, *Penal Legislation,* pp. 191-192.

[23] Canon 2251.

[24] Canon 2248: 1.

[25] Canon 2236: 1.

tion for the wrong he has done and the scandal he has given.[26] A censure imposed by the Holy See or reserved to it by law can be absolved only by the Holy See,[27] or by one legitimately delegated by that authority, either " per modum habitus " or " per modum actus ", to absolve from the censure.

The censure of Canon 2335 is reserved *simply* i. e., *simpliciter,* to the Holy See: in ordinary circumstances it can be absolved only by the Holy See or someone empowered by the Holy See to do so: in extraordinary circumstances delegation is granted *a jure* by Canons 882 and 2254.

To absolve a Mason or a member of a similar society from censure the conditions must always be fulfilled, whether the absolution is granted by the Sacred Penitentiary, or the Apostolic Delegate, or by the Bishop, or Confessor, enjoying the Pagella.[28] The first condition is *regularly* to be demanded.[29] Whilst it is true a confessor cannot licitly or validly absolve a Mason who persists in retaining membership in his lodge, still the Holy Office allowed that such a one retain membership if he could not withdraw *absque gravi damno*.[30]

What sort of abjuration is to be demanded? *Per se* formal abjuration is unnecessary. This the Holy Office at least tacitly declared, August 3, 1898: The Bishop of N. asked if the *eiurent* of the Pagella should be judicial abjuration. and the Holy Office allowed that the penitents " saltem coram confessario eiurent, seu detestantur." They should promise, Vermeersch points out, after the decree of March 7, 1883, " numquam amplius fore ut sese immisceant alicui actui societatum ipsarum tum secreto tum publico, et

[26] Cf. Canon 2248: 2, and Canon 2242: 2.
[27] Cf. Canon 7.
[28] Cf. S. C. S. Off., 3 Aug., 1898, *C. I. C. Fontes,* IV, p. 504, No. 1204.
[29] Genicot-Salsmans, *Inst. Theo. Mor.,* II, 561, No. 594.
[30] S. C. S. Off., 7 Martii, 1883, *Collectanea S. C. P. F.,* II, p. 82.

praesertim numquam se soluturos requisitam contributionem ".[31]   The separation from the society should extend even to the exclusion of Masonic funeral rites or other non-Catholic rites at the time of death.[32]

The second condition, that of denouncing to the Holy Office all clerics and religious known to be members of the censured societies, can be fulfilled either personally by the penitent by letter, or through the confessor, or the Ordinary. It is no longer necessary, as has already been seen, to denounce ordinary members, *fautores,* or *occultos duces ac coriphaeos.*

The third condition demands that the books, manuscripts, and insignia be turned over to the confessor for transmission to the Holy Office, of course, through the Ordinary.   For grave and just reasons, e. g., for fear that they would fall into the hands of those they would harm, it is sufficient that the confessor burn them.   It would also seem permissible that the penitent himself destroy them, if their delivery to the priest would entail grave inconvenience.

The fourth condition demands a fitting penance be inflicted on the penitent together with frequent confession, and that the scandal be repaired.   Public confession and communion would seem to be adequate reparation where the penitent is known.[33]

In a case of urgent necessity, e. g., if the censure of canon 2335 cannot be externally observed without danger of grave scandal or infamy, or if it would be hard for the newly converted penitent to remain in mortal sin, either v. g., because he has been making a mission, retreat, or the like, or for any other sufficient reason, until the competent Superior be ap-

---

[31] Vermeersch-Creusen, III, p. 277, No. 535; *Collectanea S. C. P. F.,* II, p. 182, No. 1593.

[32] Vermeersch-Creusen, III, p. 277, No. 535.

[33] Cf. Noldin, *Sum. Theo. Mor.,* II, p. 130, No. 115.

proached, viz., the Sacred Penitentiary, or the Apostolic Delegate, or a bishop, or confessor who enjoys the Pagella, any confessor can absolve in the act of sacramental confession from the censure, on condition that the penitent have recourse, personally, or through the confessor and by letter, " reticito nomine " to a competent authority. The recourse must be had within a month, and the penitent must observe the command of the Superior, under pain of having the censure recur.[34]

The penitent is free, however, even after absolution, and having had recourse to the proper Superior, to go to another Confessor who has the faculty, and, having confessed the offense for which he incurred excommunication, obtain absolution. Absolution obtained, and the penance imposed by the Confessor accepted, the penitent need not obey the command coming from the Superior to whom he previously had recourse.[35]

If, however, recourse is morally impossible, the Confessor can absolve the Mason without the necessity of having recourse to the proper Superior, under the prescribed conditions, and having imposed a fitting penance, and satisfaction for the censure, to be performed within a definite time, under pain of having the censure recur. The prescribed conditions are those contained in the Pagella. They are also to be demanded by the Superior to whom recourse has been taken, for he has his faculties also under the conditions expressed in the Pagella, " ita tamen ", etc.[36]

It is enough, for valid and licit absolution from the censure " ad normam Canonis 882 " that the penitent have at least the intention of quitting the society.

[34] Canon 2254: 1.
[35] Canon 2254: 2.
[36] Hilling, *C. I. C. Supplementum*, p. 51, No. v.

Corollary.

Concerning the absolution of members of merely secret societies, the Third Plenary Council of Baltimore has decreed the following:—all members of societies that demand an oath of secrecy or of strict obedience cannot be absolved until they effectually quit the society or seriously promise to do so.[37] Absolution from the sin incurred by joining other societies condemned without censure, would, surely, be given on the same conditions.

ARTICLE II.   PASSIVE MEMBERSHIP IN CERTAIN CONDEMNED

SOCIETIES

After the formal condemnation of the three American Secret Societies that are not under censure, viz., the Odd Fellows, the Sons of Temperance and the Knights of Pythias, by the Sacred Congregation of the Holy Office, August 20, 1894,[1] many of the Bishops of the United States asked the Holy See " An aliquid hac in re permitti possit? " [2] It seems that many Catholics had joined these societies in good faith and, " erogata modica pecuniae summa ad instar taxae temporibus statutis solvendae jus acquirant ad longe majora subsidia sive pro se casibus infirmitatis aut necessitatis, sive pro familia mortis casu." [3]   To have stopped these payments would in no way have injured the societies in question, but would have meant a considerable loss for the members compelled to withdraw by the Holy See, for " aliquando contingit ut quis obligatione in forma juris valida teneatur de aere alieno statis pensionibus solvendi, quin totum in praesens restituere possit." [4]

[37] *Conc. Plen. Balt. III, Acta et Decreta,* Tit. VIII, cap. III, No. 1, n. 247.

[1] *Acta Sanctae Sedis,* XXVIII, p. 569.

[2] S. C. S. Off., Jan. 18, 1896, *Eccl. Review,* 14, p. 361.

[3] S. C. S. Off., Jan. 18, *Eccl. Review,* 14, p. 361.

[4] S. C. S. Off., Jan. 18, 1896, *Eccl. Review,* 14, p. 361.

The Holy Father, Pope Leo XIII, entrusted the examination of this difficult matter to the Holy Office, and the Congregation decided " Generatim loquendo, non licere." It was the mind of the Holy Office that it could be tolerated under the following conditions: [5]—(1) that they joined the society in good faith before knowing that it was condemned; (2) that no scandal result therefrom or that it be removed by declaring that the only reason for retaining membership is not to incur material losses, and meanwhile all communication with the sect be avoided and the meetings not attended; (3) that it be impossible to withdraw without grave loss; (4) that there be no danger of perversion for the party himself or his family, particularly in the case of sickness or of death, nor danger of a non-Catholic funeral. To all this the Pontiff added: " Cum de re gravissima atque periculorum et difficultatum plena agitur, quae plurimas non modo dioecesas, sed et provincias ecclesiasticas respicit, ut uniformis regulae servandae causa, impletis omnibus quae hac decreto statuuntur, casibus particularibus. . . . Eminentia Tua et in Apostolica Delegatione Successores providere possit.[6]

There soon arose, however, a question as to whether every case was to be referred to the Apostolic Delegate. The Editor of the *Ecclesiastical Review*[7] commenting upon the above-mentioned decree, wrote in part: " When all the conditions are verified in one case, the confessor, or the pastor, or the bishop, has sufficient cause for making application in order to obtain permission to give absolution to a person who allows his name to remain on the membership list of the society for the purpose of holding a sort of legal title to

---

[5] *A. S. S.*, XXVII, p. 699; English version from Ayrinhac, *Penal Legislation*, etc., p. 243.

[6] *Acta Sanctae Sedis*, XXVIII, 699.

[7] *Eccl. Review*, XIV, p. 472.

certain temporal benefits towards the creation of which he had advanced money.   Similar cases would be those in which a person has borrowed money from a society to be repaid by installment, or in the form of dues. . . . "

Meanwhile a discussion took place as to the meaning of the phrase " in casibus particularibus " [8] which was finally concluded by a declaration of the Apostolic Delegate, Cardinal Satolli, that the letter meant " in singulis casibus ", and that it was necessary in every case to apply to the Apostolic Delegate for permission to remain a member of these societies.

It was certain, then, that in every case recourse was to be had to the Apostolic Delegate for permission to retain passive membership in these societies, when all the four conditions laid down by the Holy See were fulfilled.

About a score of years later, at the instance of the Cardinal Archbishop of Baltimore, the Sacred Congregation of the Holy Office, June 26, 1913, extended this faculty to all the Archbishops of the United States.   The American Bishops had represented to the Holy See, through Cardinal Gibbons, that, since it was necessary in nearly every case to consult the Ordinary as to the details of such cases occurring in his jurisdiction, it would simplify matters if the faculty were extended to all the Bishops of the country.   The Holy Office compromised by extending the faculty, not to the Bishops, but to the Metropolitans for their several provinces. The decree is in part as follows:

Firmis manentibus facultatibus Delegati Apostolici, supplicandum Ssmo pro extensione facultatis ad singulos Archiepiscopos ad unumquemque pro sua respectiva provincia, servatis prorsus conditionibus decreti feriae IV diei 19 Januarii, 1896, *onerata eorum conscientia*.   Et sequenti feria V die 27 ejusdem

[8] Cf. Sabetti, *Compendium Theologiae Moralis*, ed. 12 (1896), p. 782; *Amer. Cath. Quarterly Review*, Oct. 1896, p. 890; *Eccl. Review*, 14, p. 470 and 15, p. 638.

mensis junii, Sanctitas Sua petitionem juxta E'morum et R'morum Patrum suffragia benigne concessit.[9]

What is the application of this dispensation for passive membership, and what are the conditions under which it is obtained? The following is the questionnaire sent by the Apostolic Delegate to a priest making application for a penitent, and might well be used by a metropolitan chancery:—

Reverend and dear Sir:—

Before I can take into consideration the application of Mr. .... for a dispensation to remain a passive member of the society of .... the following questions must be answered and signed by the petitioner:

1. Give full name and surname ....
2. Give the name of the prohibited Society ....
3. Give the date of entrance into said Society ....
4. Did you enter the Society in good faith?
5. Is there any scandal in your remaining in said society as a passive member?
6. Give financial loss consequent upon withdrawal from said society ....
7. Will you abstain from all communication with, and never assist at any meetings of said society? ....
8. Is there any danger of perversion from Catholic faith and practise for yourself or family, from your remaining in said society? ....
9. Will you make provision that, in case of death, you will be buried with the rites of the Catholic Church only? ....

N. B. If the Society was entered after the condemnation, a sworn statement, *made in the presence of the priest,* attesting the good faith of the petitioner at the time of entrance, is required.

Sincerely yours in Christ,

N ....[10]

---

[9] *Eccl. Review,* 49, p. 468.

[10] Blank Questionnaire obtained from Apostolic Delegation.

On examining this questionnaire it will be seen that the second question is to determine whether or not the society in question is one in which the Church will allow passive membership " per modum exceptionis ". The third and fourth, with the note on question three, are to ascertain the good faith of the member, the first condition laid down in the faculty granted first to the Apostolic Delegate, and then to the Metropolitans of the country.[11] The fifth question was necessitated by the second condition of the decree.[12] The sixth question [13] is concerned with the third condition.[14] Finally, the eighth and ninth questions are relative to the fourth condition.[15]

As to the application of this faculty there are three cases in which good faith can be verified: first, in one who joined these societies before their condemnation, August 20, 1894: [16] second, in a Catholic who joined these societies after their condemnation, but ignorant of it: [17] third, in a non-Catholic

---

[11] *A. S. S.*, XXVIII, p. 699, No. 1:—" Si bona fides sectae primitus dederit, antequam sibi innotuisset, societatem fuisse damnatam."

[12] *A. S. S.*, XXVIII, p. 699, No. 2: — " Si absit scandalum, vel opportune removeatur declaratione, id a se fieri, ne jus ad emolumenta vel beneficium temporis in aere alieno solvendo amittat a quavis interim sectae communione et a quovis interventu, etiam materiali ut praemittur abstinendo."

[13] *A. S. S.*, XXVIII, p. 699, No. 3:—" si grave damnum sibi aut familiae in renunciatione obveniat."

[14] *A. S. S.*, XXVIII, p. 699, No. 2:—" Si absit etc."

[15] *A. S. S.*, XXVIII, p. 699, No. 4: — " Tandem ut non adsit vel homini illi, vel familiae ejus periculum perversionis e parte sectariorum spectato praecipue casu vel infirmitatis vel mortis, neve similiter adsit periculum funeris peragendi, a ritibus catholicis alieni."

[16] S. C. S. Off., Aug. 20, 1894; *A. S. S.*, XXVIII, p. 569.

[17] Cf. Questionnaire sent out by the Apostolic Delegate, given above, in which is read, in the note on question three: " N. B. If the society was entered after the condemnation, a sworn statement made in the presence of the priest, attesting the good faith of the petitioner at time of entrance, is required."

who is converted to the Church, and who had joined these societies while a non-Catholic.[18]

The second condition, " Si absit scandalum ", etc., is self-explanatory. There would be no scandal present, if the fact that the petitioner was a member of these secret societies was not known, or if the people of the locality were not ignorant that passive membership in these societies was allowed by the Holy See under certain conditions. Scandal, if it were likely to occur, could be removed " by an adequate statement . . . to the effect that membership was allowed solely for the purpose of obtaining the benefits to which the member is entitled in equity; and that such a member has no intention of participating in the activities of the Society by attending its regular meetings." [19]

The third condition is readily understood. To suffer the loss of benefits by complete renunciation would be a grave inconvenience to the greater majority of the members of such societies in the event of sickness, or other dire necessity, as would the loss of the insurance be to their families in the event of death. Similarly, to have a mortgage held against his home or property by the societies concerned foreclosed on his withdrawal from the society, or to have securities valuable to him only as a member of the society become worthless by his leaving the society, would work a great hardship on the average member.

The first part of the fourth condition will be fulfilled if the member fulfill the second; one could receive sick benefits without being perverted again to the forbidden society. The clause concerning the danger of a non-Catholic funeral can be taken care of either by verbal direction of the member to whosoever would be likely to be in charge of the funeral, or by request in his will.

[18] *The Casuist*, vol. II, p. 48.
[19] *Eccl. Review*, 49, p. 471.

If, according to the judgment of the Apostolic Delegate, the four conditions are fulfilled, the following faculty is sent by the chancery of the Apostolic Delegation to the priest making the petition, enabling him to permit the member to retain passive membership :—

Mr. .... has been know to this Apostolic Delegation (or Metropolitan Chancery), that he joined the Society of .... in good faith in the year .... Now, however, he asks that he be permitted to retain a passive membership is said society, for the following reasons : ....

Having, therefore, carefully considered the matter, and in virtue of the faculties conceded to the Apostolic Delegate by the Holy See on the 18th day of January, 1896, namely, that he " may provide for particular cases ", we grant power to the .... to permit the petitioner to leave his name on the rolls, and to continue to pay his taxes or debts, to the said Society, provided that the circumstances of the case have been truthfully stated, and under the following conditions :

1. That there be no cause of scandal, or that such scandal be removed by a timely declaration that said passive membership is retained only in order that the benefits to which the petitioner is entitled be not lost to him.

2. That at the same time, the petitioner refrain from all communication with, and even from any material intervention in the affairs of the Society.

3. That there be no danger of preversion to the petitioner, or to his family, especially in the event of sickness, or death, and that there shall be in the funeral services nothing which is not in accordance with the rubrics of the Catholic Church.

4. That the payment of the taxes or debts be acquitted through the intermediary of another person, or by mail, so that the petitioner will, in no way, assist at any meeting of said Society.

Given at Washington, D. C.
  At the Apostolic Delegation,

N ....

192–   Apostolic Delegate (or Archbishop of N—)[20]

It will be noted in the foregoing faculty that this dispensation, like all others, is only " si preces nituntur veritati." [21] It will also be noted that this document brings out what is found nowhere else, that the dues, or installments on mortgages, or loans, are to be paid not by the person himself at the meetings, but through a second person, or by mail.

This formula might also be well used by a Metropolitan faculty to which a similar application was made.

[20] Cf. Blank formula obtained from the Apostolic Delegation.
[21] Cf. Canon 40.

BIBLIOGRAPHY

Sources

Codex Iuris Canonici, Pii X Pontificis Maximi Iussu Digestus, Benedicti Papae XV Auctoritate Promulgatus, Romae, 1917.

Acta Apostolicae Sedis, 19 vols. Romae, 1909–.

Acta et Decreta Conc. Plen. Balt. III. Baltimorae, 1886.

Acta Leonis XIII Pontificis Maximi, 22 vols. Romae, 1881-1893.

Acta Pii IX, 7 vols. Romae, n. d.

Acta Sanctae Sedis, 41 vols. Romae, 1865-1908.

Bullarii Romani Continuatio, 14 vols. Prati, 1845-1866.

Canones et Decreta Sacrosancti Oecumenici Concilii Tridentini. Taurini, 1913.

Codex Iuris Canonici . . . Praefatione, Fontium Annotatione et Indice Analytico-Alphabetico ab E'mo Petro Card. Gasparri Auctus. Romae, 1918.

Codicis Iuris Canonici Fontes (C. I. C. Fontes), Cura E'mi Petri Card. Gasparri Editi, 4 vols. Romae, 1923-1926.

Collectanea Sacrae Congregationis de Propaganda Fide, seu Decreta, Instructiones, Rescripta Pro Apostolicis Missionibus. 2 vols. Romae, 1907.

Concilii Plen. Balt. II Acta et Decreta. Baltimorae, 1868.

Concilia Provincialia Baltimorae Habita 1829-1840. Baltimorae, 1842.

Constitutiones Sacri Ordinis Praedicatorum, Constitutio No. 35, Acta et Decreta Capituli Generalis Provincialium. Romae, 1924.

Corpus Iuris Canonici, ed. *Lipsiensis secunda post Aemilii Ludovici Richerti curas ad librorum manuscriptorum et editionis romanae fidem recognovit et adnotatione critica instruxit Aemilius Friedburg,* 2 vols. Lipsiae, 1922.

de Martinis, *Iuris Pontificii de Propaganda Fide (Partes),* 7 vols. Romae, 1888-1895.

Denzinger-Bannwert, *Enchiridion Symbolorum, Definitionum et Declarationum de Rebus Fidei et Morum,* ed. 13a. Friburgi Brisgoviae, 1921.

Index Librorum Prohibitorum, S'mi D. N. Pii IX Pont. Max. Iussu Editus. Romae, 1877.

Index Librorum Prohibitorum Leonis XIII S. P. Auctoritate Recognitus, S'mi D. N. Pii PP. XI. Iussu Editus. Romae, 1922.

Mansi, *Sacrorum Conciliorum Nova et Amplissima Collectio,* 51 vols. Paris, 1901–.

Migne, *Patrologia Latina,* 221 vols. Parisiis, 1847-1870.

PERIODICALS

American Catholic Historical Review. Philadelphia, 1884-1927.

American Catholic Quarterly Review. Philadelphia, 1876–.

American Ecclesiastical Review (A. E. R.). Philadelphia, 1889-1927.

Irish Ecclesiastical Record (I. E. R.). Dublin, 1865-1927.

Tablet, The London, 149 vols. London, 1853-1927.

Theologisch-Practische Quartal Schrift, Linz, 79 vols. 1847-1927.

Vermeersch, *De Religiosis et Missionariis Supplementa et Monumenta Periodica,* 14 vols. Brugis, 1911-1926.

REPERTORIES

Catholic Encyclopedia, 17 vols. New York, 1907-1922.

Dictionnaire Apologétique de la Foi Catholique, I–. Paris, 1912–.

Hastings, *Encyclopedia of Religion and Ethics,* 12 vols. New York, 1908-1922.

Kirchenlexikon, Wetzer und Welte's, 12 vols. and *Register,* Freiburg, im Brisgau, 1886-1903.

AUTHORITIES

a Coronata, *De Locis et Temporibus Sacris.* Augustae Taurinorum, 1922.

Aertnys, *Theologia Moralis Iuxta Doctrinam S. Alphonsi de Ligorio,* 2 vols. Tornaci, 1893.

Aichner, *Compendium Iuris Ecclesiastici,* ed. 6a. Brixinae, 1887.

Alzog, *Manual of Universal Church History,* 3 vols. Cincinnati, 1878.

Arregui, *Summarium Theologiae Moralis.* Bilboa, 1923.

Augustine, *A Commentary on the New Code of Canon Law,* 8 vols. St. Louis and London, 1918-1922.

Augustine, *The Rights and Duties of Ordinaries.* St. Louis and London, 1924.

Avazini, *De Constitutione Apostolicae Sedis Commentarium.* Romae, 1874.

Ayrinhac, *Marriage Legislation in the New Code of Canon Law.* New York, Cincinnati and Chicago, 1919.

——, *Penal Legislation in the New Code of Canon Law.* New York, Cincinnati and Chicago, 1920.

Ballerini-Palmieri, *Opus Theologicum Morale,* 7 vols. Prati, 1893.

Bargilliat, *Praelectiones Iuris Canonici,* ed. 24a., 2 vols. Parisiis, 1907.

——, *Praelectiones Iuris Canonici,* ed. 37a., 2 vols. Parisiis, 1923.

Bouuaert-Simenon, *Manuale Iuris Canonici, Ad Usum Seminariorum.* Gandae et Leodii, 1922.

Blat, *Commentarium Codicis Iuris Canonici,* ed. 2a., 5 vols. Romae, 1924.

Bucceroni, *Institutiones Theologiae Moralis,* ed. 6a., 4 vols. Romae, 1915.

Cappello, *De Censuris, Tractatus Canonico-Moralis Iuxta C. I. C.,* ed. 2a. Taurinorum Augustae, 1925.

——, *De Sacramentis, Tractatus Canonico-Moralis Iuxta C. I. C.,* 3 vols. Taurinorum Augustae, 1923.

Carr, *The Constitution Apostolicae Sedis Moderationi Explained,* 2 vols. Dublin, 1879.

Casuist, The, vols. I–. New York, 1906–.

Cerato, *Censurae Vigentes Ipso Facto a Codice Iuris Canonici Excerptae, Commentarium,* ed. 3. Patavii, 1921.

——, *Matrimonium a Codice Iuris Canonici Integre Desumptum,* Patavii, 1920.

Chelodi, *Ius Matrimoniale.* Tridentini, 1921.

——, *Ius De Personis.* Tridentini, 1922.

——, *Ius Poenale et Ordo in Iudiciis Criminalibus Iuxta C. I. C.,* Tridentini, 1925.

Christopher, *S. Aurelii Augustini de Catechizandis Rudibus Liber Unus, A Translation with Commentary.* Washington, 1926.

Cicognani, *Ius Canonicum Primo Studii Anno in Usum Auditorum Excerpta, Commentarium Libri Primi Codicis,* 2 vols. Romae, 1925.

Cippolini, *De Censuris Latae Sententiae Iuxta C. I. C.* Taurinorum Augustae, 1920.

Cocchi, *Commentarium in Codicem Iuris Canonici,* ed. 2a., 8 vols. Taurinorum Augustae, 1926.

Cooper, *Freemasonry,* reprint from *Ecclesiastical Review.* Philadelphia, 1917.

Crnica, *Modificationes in Tractatu de Censuris per Codicem Iuris Canonici Introductae,* S. Mauritii Agaunensis, 1919.

d'Annibale, *Summula Theologiae Moralis,* ed. 3a., 3 vols. Romae, 1892.

Darras, *A General History of the Catholic Church,* 4 vols. New York, 1865.

de Becker, *Praelectiones Canonicae de Sponsalibus et Matrimonio,* ed. 2a. Louvanii, New York, 1903.

Demeuran, *Le Droit Canonique des Läiques, d'après le Nouveau Code.* Paris, 1919.

Deshayes, *Memento Iuris Ecclesiastici Publici et Privati.* Parisiis, 1895.

de Smet, *De Sponsalibus et Matrimonio,* ed. 1. Brugis, 1909.

——, *De Sponsalibus et Matrimonio,* ad Normam Codicis Recognita, ed. 4a., 2 vols. Brugis, 1923.

Dwight, *Centennial History of the American Bible Society,* 2 vols. New York, 1916.

Eichmann, *Das Strafrecht nach der Codex Iuris Canonici.* Paderborn, 1920.

Fagnanus, *Commentarium in V. Libros Decretalium.* Venetiis, 1729.

Fanfani, *De Iure Religiosorum, ad Normam C. I. C.* Taurini, Romae, 1925.

Farrugia, *Commentarium in Censuras Latae Sententiae C. I. C.,* ed. 2a. Melitae, 1921.

——, *De Matrimonio et Causis Matrimonialibus, Tractatus Canonico-Moralis Iuxta C. I. C.* Taurini, Romae, 1924.

Ferreres, *Compendium Theologiae Moralis,* ed. 13a., 2 vols. (6a. post Cod.). Barcinone, 1925.

——, *Institutiones Canonicae,* ed. 2a., 2 vols. Barcinone, 1920.

Gasparri, *Codicis Iuris Canonici Fontes,* 4 vols. Romae, 1923-1926.

——, *De Matrimonio, Tractatus Canonicus,* 2 vols. Parisiis, 1904.

——, *De Ordinatione, Tractatus Canonicus,* 2 vols. Parisiis, 1893.

Genicot, *Institutiones Theologiae Moralis,* 2 vols. Lovanii, 1896.

Genicot–Salsmans, *Institutiones Theologiae Moralis,* ed. 10a., 2 vols. Bruxellis, 1922.

Gennari, *Quistioni Teologico-Morali.* Roma, 1907.

Godfrey, *The Right of Patronage in the New Code of Canon Law.* Washington, 1924.

Hillings, *Codicis Iuris Canonici Supplementum.* Friburgi Brisgoviae, 1925.

Kearney, *Sponsors at Baptism.* Washington, 1925.

Könings, *Commentarium in Facultates Apostolicas.* Neo-Eboraci, Cincinnati, S. Ludovici, Einsidlae, 1884.

——, *Theologia Moralis Novissimi Doctoris S. Alphonsi,* ed. 7a., 2 vols. Neo-Eboraci, Cincinnati, Einsidlae, 1889.

Lega, *Praelectiones in Text. Iur. Can.,* ed. 2a., 4 vols. Romae, 1905.

Lehmkuhl, *Casus Conscientiae.* Friburgi Brisgoviae, 1913.

——, *Theologia Moralis,* ed. 5a., 2 vols. Friburgi Brisgoviae, 1888.

——, *Theologia Moralis,* ed. 24a., 2 vols. Friburgi Brisgoviae, 1915.

Liguori, S. Alphonsus, *Doc. Ecc.,* ed. Haringer, 8 vols. Ratisbonae, 1880.

Marc, *Institutiones Morales Alphonsianae,* 2 vols. Romae, 1885.

Mothon, *Institutions Canoniques, a l'Usage des Curies Episcopales, de Clerge Parroissial, et des Familles Religieuses,* 2 vols. Lille, Bruges, 1924.

Motry, *Diocesan Faculties.* Washington, 1921.

Nilles, *Commentaria in Con. Plen. Balt. III,* 2 vols. Oeniponte, 1890.

Noldin, *De Poenis Ecclesiasticis,* ed. 7a. Oeniponte, 1907.

——, *Summa Theologiae Moralis,* 3 vols., ed. 7a. Oeniponte, 1907.

Noldin–Schöneger, *De Poenis Ecclesiasticis,* ed. 14a. Oeniponte, 1923.

——, *Summa Theologiae Moralis,* ed. 14a. Oeniponte, 1923.

O'Connor, *Foreign Freemasonry.* Philadelphia, 1901.

O'Leary, *Recollections of Fenians and Fenianism,* 2 vols. London, 1896.

Pennacchi, *Commentaria in Constitutionem "Apostolicae Sedis",* 2 vols. Romae, 1883.

Pesch, *Compendium Theologiae Dogmaticae,* ed. 2a., 4 vols. Friburgi, Brisgoviae, 1920-1922.

Petrovits, *The New Church Law on Marriage,* 2nd ed. Philadelphia, 1926.

Pighi, *Censurae Latae Sententiae,* ed. 5a. Veroniae, 1919.

Pistocchi, *I Canoni Penali del Codice Ecclesiastico, Espositi e Commentati.* Torino–Romae, 1925.

Pollard, *The Secret Societies of Ireland.* London, 1922.

Preuss, *A Dictionary of Secret and Other Societies.* St. Louis and London, 1923.

——, *A Study of American Freemasonry.* St. Louis and London, 1908.

Prümmer, *Manuale Iuris Canonici,* ed. 3a. Friburgi Brisgoviae, 1922.

——, *Manuale Theologiae Moralis,* ed. 3a., 3 vols. Friburgi Brisgoviae, 1923.

Putzer, *Commentarium in Facultates Apostolicas,* ed. 3a. Ilchestrae, 1893.

Rohling, *Medulla Theologiae Moralis.* S. Ludovici, 1875.

Rosen, *The Catholic Church and Secret Societies.* Milwaukee, 1902.

Sabetti, *Compendium Theologiae Moralis,* ed. 12a. Neo-Eboraci et Cincinnati, 1896.

Sabetti-Barrett, *Compendium Theologiae Moralis,* ed. 19a. Neo-Eboraci, 1920.

Savage, *Fenian Heroes and Martyrs.* Boston, 1868.

Schaaf, *The Cloister.* Cincinnati, 1921.

Schäfer, *Das Eherecht nach der Codex Iuris Canonici.* Munster, 1921.

Sebastiani, *Compendium Theologiae Moralis,* ed. 2a. Augustae Taurinorum, 1918.

Simon, *Faculties of Pastors and Confessors for Absolution and Dispensation.* New York, 1922.

Slater, *Cases of Conscience,* 2 vols. New York, Cincinnati and Chicago, 1912.

——, *A Manual of Moral Theology,* 2 vols. New York, 1918.

Smith, *Notes on the Second Plenary Council of Baltimore.* New York, 1874.

Sole, *De Delictis et Poenis.* Romae, 1920.

Tanquerey, *Synopsis Theologiae Moralis et Pastoralis,* ed. 7a., 3 vols. Romae, 1922.

Thépany, *Constitution Apostolicae Sedis Commentaire.* Tours, 1883.

Telch, *Epitome Theologiae Moralis Universae.* Oeniponte, Ratisbonae, Romae, Neo-Eboraci et Cincinnati, 1920.

Vermeersch-Creusen, *Epitome Iuris Canonici,* ed. 2a., 3 vols. Mechlinae, Romae, 1924-1925.

Vermeersch, *De Prohibitione et Censura Librorum,* ed. 2a. Romae, 1898.

Vlaming, *Praelectiones Iuris Matrimonii,* ed. 3a., 2 vols. Bussum in Hollandia, 1919.

Wernz, *Ius Decretalium,* ed. 3a., 6 vols. Prati, 1915.

Wernz–Vidal, *Ius Canonicum,* vols. II and V. Romae, 1923-1925.

Woywod, *A Practical Commentary on the New Code of Canon Law,* ed. 2a., 2 vols. New York, 1925-1926.

Universitas Catholica Americae

Washington, D. C.

Facultas Juris Canonici

1926–1927

No. 46

DEUS LUX MEA

THESES

QUAS

AD DOCTORATUS GRADUM

IN IURE CANONICO

APUD UNIVERSITATEM CATHOLICAM AMERICAE

CONSEQUENDUM
PUBLICE PROPUGNABIT

IOSEPHUS ANTONIUS MICHAELIS QUIGLEY

SACERDOS ARCHIDIOECESEOS PHILADELPHIENSIS

BACCALAUREUS ARTIUM

ET

LICENTIATUS IN IURE CANONICO

HORA IX A. M. DIE XXVIII MAII A. D. MCMXXVII

IUS CANONICUM

ROMAN LAW

INTERNATIONAL LAW

LII. Nature and Sources of International Law
LIII. State Rights
LIV. Treaties, Their Purpose and Scope
LV. The Monroe Doctrine
LVI. The Drago Doctrine
LVII. Arbitration
LVIII. Diplomatic Agents and Consuls
LIX. Protectorates, Mandates, Suzerainties and Spheres of Influence

DISSERTATION

LX. Condemned Societies

Vidit Facultas Iuris Canonici:

PHILIPPUS BERNARDINI, S.T.D., J.U.D., *Decanus*
LUDOVICUS H. MOTRY, S.T.D., J.C.D., *a Secretis*
VALENTINUS T. SCHAAF, O.F.M., S.T.B., J.C.D.
FRANCISCUS LARDONE, S.T.D., J.U.D.
MANOEL DE OLIVIERA LIMA, LL.D., L.H.B.

Vidit Rector:

THOMAS J. SHAHAN, S.T.D., J.U.D.

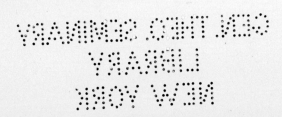

BIOGRAPHICAL NOTE

JOSEPH A. M. QUIGLEY was born in Philadelphia, May 11, 1900. After having completed his primary and secondary education, he entered St. Charles Seminary, Overbrook, September 4, 1917, and was ordained to the Holy Priesthood, June 6, 1925. In the fall of that year he began graduate studies in the School of Canon Law at the Catholic University.